P9-DHT-872

BEYOND CHAOS — LIVING THE
CHRISTIAN FAMILY IN A
WORLD LIKE OURS

BEYOND CHAOS — Living the Christian Family in a World Like Ours

Chris William Erdman

WILLIAM B. EERDMANS PUBLISHING COMPANY
GRAND RAPIDS, MICHIGAN / CAMBRIDGE, U.K.

© 1996 Chris William Erdman

Published by Wm. B. Eerdmans Publishing Co.
255 Jefferson Ave. S.E., Grand Rapids, Michigan 49503 /
P.O. Box 163, Cambridge CB3 9PU U.K.
All rights reserved

Printed in the United States of America

01 00 99 98 97 96   7 6 5 4 3 2 1

Library of Congress Cataloging-in-Publication Data

Erdman, Chris William.
    Beyond chaos — living the Christian family in a world like ours /
Chris William Erdman.
        p.   cm.
    Includes bibliographical references
    ISBN 0-8028-4130-9 (pbk.: alk. paper)
    1. Family — Religious aspects — Christianity. 2. Family — Religious life.
I. Title
BV4526.2.E73   1996
261.8'3585 — dc20   96-7911
                                                       CIP

Unless otherwise noted, the Scripture quotations contained herein are from the New Revised Standard Version of the Bible, copyright © 1989 by the Division of Christian Education of the National Council of Churches of Christ in the U.S.A., and are used by permission. All rights reserved.

For
Julie,
Joshua,
and
Jeremy

Contents

CONTENTS

Preface

"Please read this first!" These big, bold words greeted me as I opened the box containing my boys' first swing set. I bought it while my wife Julie and the boys were away visiting her family in California. I hoped to surprise them when they returned.

Driving home from Wal-Mart, I could almost see their eyes grow big with excitement when they spied the structure of metal and plastic in the backyard. I was eager to have the thing together . . . too eager.

Because my list of spring chores was rather long, and didn't allow for much wasted time, I dove into the project. Assembly looked simple enough — insert a metal tube here, attach a bar there. The important instruction packet, with that bold warning emblazoned on the first page, went unused . . . until I got stuck. I reached a point where nothing made sense. The only way to make one tube fit into another was by persuasion . . . my hammer. And once in place, the whole section wasn't square.

In desperation I tore open the *"Please read this first!"* instruction packet. Within a few moments I realized my error. Failing to see the big picture, I'd jumped in at the wrong place, and missed a half-dozen important steps. What could have taken me two hours, took me four. I found myself hoping the neighbor wasn't watching.

That instruction packet would have been a handy guide.

Consider this Preface such a guide. I hope these few paragraphs will help you see the big picture.

This book bears a message. Each sentence, paragraph, and chapter serves as an element of that message. Like me, in my eagerness to assemble my sons' swing set, some readers may be tempted to skip over the important material in the first two sections of this book in their haste to get to the chapters in the last section. If they do, they won't fully understand the implications of the final chapters. Here's why . . .

Part One: The Family Faces a Changing World, introduces some of the sweeping changes facing American Christians and their families today; it also identifies possible reasons for what some are calling a revolution of American family life.

Next, by introducing three biblical metaphors, *Part Two: The Family Recovers Its Identity* attempts to reinvigorate a sense of Christian identity in an America no longer shaped by the Judeo-Christian religious tradition. *Exile* calls readers to acknowledge the danger of an uncritical assimilation into American culture. *Babylon* helps readers name and resist the idolatrous powers prevalent in today's America. And *Exodus* urges readers out of a religious ghetto and into American society in evangelical mission.

With these first two sections as a foundation, *Part Three: The Family Engages God's World*, suggests some practical ways to transform the ordinary aspects of family life in light of the mission of Jesus Christ through the local church. I address only a few. For example, I discuss the way we ought to view money, encouraging lifestyles more faithful to Jesus Christ than to the assumptions of Madison Avenue, Hollywood, or Washington, D.C., but I don't address other important areas like work and vocation. My discussion isn't meant to be exhaustive, but it is meant to be suggestive. I hope that the book's message will help you to identify other areas in need of transformation and, under God's guidance, to find creative ways to make the changes. The rest of the book is yours to write.

Some readers may find my focus on the church strange in a discussion of the family. That merely reveals how far we American Christians have strayed. Any authentically Christian vision and ethic of family life depends upon a broader vision and ethic of the church. The family is not an independent entity. Understood properly, the family is an expression of faithfulness to God and gospel and kingdom. Families must learn to define themselves by the gospel story in such a way that they can tell that story as members of local Christian congregations, and conduct their lives in such a way that they embody the truth of the story. I hope this book helps to transform families into witnesses to the good news of God's justice and salvation revealed in Jesus Christ through the power of the Holy Spirit.

A number of people deserve a warm "thank you!" for their help in this project. Not all of them agree with what I suggest, but each of them contributed in some way to the finished product. Walter Brueggemann, Dale Bruner, Stanley Hauerwas, George Hunsberger, Richard Mouw, William Willimon, and my colleagues in the *Gospel and Our Culture Network* all provided important direction, encouragement, and challenge at various stages in this project. Chip Ricks provided invaluable tips for this fledgling writer, Michelle Krouse's education and expertise proved invaluable, and Bill Eerdmans and his staff made the project a reality. In addition to these, valued friends Bud and Gerry Charlton, and Wally and Cy King, read and commented on the manuscript. So did my wife's parents, Jerry and Linda Simpson. David Dawson and Carl Hofmann, whose minds and commitment to Jesus Christ I deeply admire, provided a helpful theological critique. My parents, Jim and Mardi Erdman, taught me my first words; their lives and commitment to excellence in written communication influence me more than I'll ever know.

And, of course, a special thank you to my wife Julie, my sons Joshua and Jeremy, and the saints at Covenant Presbyterian Church, Sharon, Pennsylvania. You are the ordinary heroes whose lives give texture to this book.

In many ways, this is your book. Not only is its message for you and to you — you helped write it. Your lives bear witness to the possibilities proclaimed within these pages.

As I commend this book to a larger audience, I do so in the confidence you inspire. These are not lofty thoughts divorced from the rugged realities of daily life in America's families. This book simply testifies to what I've seen God doing in our midst — transforming the lifestyles of common saints, and launching a new mission to modern America. You've proved to me that the center of this mission is not the building where the church gathers Sunday after Sunday. Instead, this mission centers on the men, women, and children scattered strategically in the homes and businesses and schools where the church's families live and work and learn each day. Like those Thessalonian believers the apostle Paul often held up for others to imitate, may your lives serve as an inspiration to believers everywhere (1 Thessalonians 1:7).

Sharon, Pennsylvania   Chris William Erdman
Pentecost 1995

PART I

THE FAMILY FACES
A CHANGING WORLD

CHAPTER 1

The Changing Look of Main Street

FLASHBACK. Dressed in their uniform white blouses, plaid skirts, and matching stockings, several girls lift their eyes from their desks. The room is quiet. Classmates work diligently on assigned lessons.

Everything in the room, and every detail of the day's schedule, is carefully planned and regimented in order to encourage reverence and submission to authority: God and country. Nonconformity is not tolerated.

The hush in the room is broken only by the scratching of the teacher's chalk on the blackboard. A daring redhead, wearing freckles and a bow, surveys the landscape. Good! With her face to the blackboard and her back to the class, the nun can't see the jester.

"What's black and white and red all over?"

A classmate giggles and whispers an answer. "A nun falling down stairs!"

The sudden burst of laughter draws an angry stare from Sister Mary Sarah.

Karen Engberg, a newspaper columnist and mother of four children, says this joke was a favorite among her classmates at the parochial school she attended in her youth. "When I tell it to my kids now," says Engberg, "I have to tell them what a nun is."[1]

Surveying the Landscape

Family Matters, Karen Engberg's weekly column, is just one voice among many wrestling with sweeping changes in American culture, more specifically in the way America understands the whole matter we call family.

Engberg's Roman Catholic schoolmates may have giggled at sacrilegious jokes, but their church was still the ark of salvation. The words of the catechism were drummed into their brains: "No salvation outside the Church." Since Protestant churches were not true churches, the girls grew up resolutely Roman Catholic.

But like their uniform school clothes, their religion did not typically express their own convictions; both dress codes and Christianity were imposed upon them. And as they grew up, many of them learned to "question authority." When finally out from under mom and dad's watchful eye, these young coeds broadened their horizons. The religion of their parents — exclusive, intolerant, archaic — was no match for their enlightened minds. Sometime during their college years, they left the church and stayed away . . . until recently.

Today, religion is "something that more and more people I know are coming back to as their children reach ages of awareness," says Engberg. She and her friends are part of a growing American religious quest.

Religion and family. For many, they go together like base-

1. Karen Engberg, "Parents Look for Meaning in Religious Stirrings," *Santa Barbara News Press* (July 12, 1992), D3.

ball and apple pie. Many of today's young parents are yesterday's religious rebels. With the arrival of children, they are forced to grapple with their past and their early religious formation. Maybe they're fed up with the self-indulgent, instant-gratification doctrines of the past thirty-something years. Maybe there's a hunger for transcendence, history, roots. Maybe the insecurity and stress of this post–cold war world kindles a quest for something old, stable, and deep. Maybe. At any rate, one thing is clear: religion must surrender to *their* terms. The religion they embrace today is very different from that which they left years ago.

Sundays, for example, for families like Engberg's, are a far cry from those she remembers as a child. The celebration in her house is a pseudoreligious ritual "of being together as a family without all the usual externally imposed schedules and deadlines." Going to church, wrestling kids through the morning routine, and trying to keep them quiet during the service all are counterproductive to her mission.

She intends to steer her family free of the rigid, orthodox indoctrination of her parents' religion. Engberg wants to raise her children to "appreciate the stories, beliefs, customs and worth" of all people. She wants her children to know the kernel of truth held in common by all religions. She will encourage them to celebrate the diversity of religious expression, without becoming dogmatic about any particular expression. Says Engberg, "You might say that my goal is to have them be read all over."

The new twist on an old pun is no laughing matter. It signals a major transformation.

For families living in Anytown, USA, materialism is now the official religion, pluralism the reigning ideology, tolerance the supreme virtue. In our public squares, any claim to absolute truth is condemned as arrogant, and any call to live responsibly in light of a particular moral tradition is dismissed as narrow-minded and old-fashioned.

A college freshman I know recently mustered up enough courage to speak up in class defending her Christian tradition's teachings regarding sexual conduct. "Intercourse is a celebration of love *and* commitment," she said, "reserved for a man and a woman bound together in the lifelong covenant of marriage." She was ridiculed by both peers and professor.

Ironically, nonconformity to the new orthodoxy (materialism, pluralism, tolerance) will not be tolerated any more than nonconformity to earlier orthodoxies was in the parochial classrooms of Engberg's youth. In its quest for freedom, our culture has cast off the constraints of the old dogmas only to be chained by the new.

It's a tough time for families that call themselves "Christian."

In the fall of 1993, Pope John Paul II issued his 10th encyclical, *Veritatis Splendor* (The Splendor of Truth). Reaffirming a traditional view of sexual ethics, the document confirms that the Pope hasn't changed his mind about things like fornication and adultery.

Were Engberg and her friends surprised? I doubt it. For many the Pope's directives were predictably rigid and intolerant, reflecting the same authoritarianism they escaped years ago.

The encyclical concerned itself with sexual morality, but at the core the Pope addressed a deeper issue: the truth. "What is truth?" asked Pontius Pilate (John 18:38). Like many around us, Pilate figured the question would free him of a bothersome discussion. After all, if truth is relative, it's a matter of personal opinion. So we're told.

And truth *is* relative. But the real question is this: relative to *what* or to *whom?* Is truth relative to our private opinions? The modern, liberal worldview? A traditional, conservative worldview? Or is it relative to God's truth spoken to Israel, revealed in Jesus Christ?

The church's bold confession, "Jesus is Lord," calls all

6

claims to the truth into question. The church knows that God's sovereignty exercised in Jesus Christ has "relativized all principalities and powers and put them under his feet."[2] Our confession will therefore always put us in an uncomfortable and somewhat confrontational position with respect to our culture.

In our world, relativism is a handy way for many of us to seek freedom at the expense of the truth. But freedom without truth is like a ship without an anchor; it sails dangerously toward the rocks. Richard John Neuhaus, reflecting on the Pope's encyclical, identifies the problem: in our "radically individualistic culture, we do not discern and obey what is objectively true. Rather, each of us decides what is 'true for me.' We *create* the truth."[3] This is a formula not for freedom, but for anarchy.

Christian families are called to stand in this cafeteria of consumer religion and morality. Jesus said, "you will know the truth, and the truth will make you free" (John 8:32). "I am the way, and the truth, and the life. No one comes to the Father except through me" (John 14:6). On his authority, whole families must learn to bear witness to the truth in this age of doubt and confusion.

Fuel for Debate

In early 1992, Vice President Dan Quayle condemned TV's Murphy Brown for having a baby out of wedlock. Some treated his remarks as a joke, another of Quayle's blunders. "Mr. Vice President," said NBC late night's David Letterman, "I don't know how to tell you this, but Murphy Brown is a fictional

2. William Willimon, *Peculiar Speech: Preaching to the Baptized* (Grand Rapids: Eerdmans, 1992), p. 92.
3. Richard John Neuhaus, "The Truth About Freedom," *The Wall Street Journal* (October 8, 1993), A14.

character."[4] He thought it was funny. I find it even more humorous, pitiful rather, that Letterman assumes fiction is simply make-believe!

Others didn't quite know what to do with Quayle's comments. Presidential hopeful Ross Perot said they were "goofy." President George Bush, rather embarrassed, ushered Canada's Brian Mulroney into a White House press conference and whispered, "I told you what the issue was, you thought I was kidding."[5]

But a large number of people took Quayle seriously.

In June 1992, senior editor Joe Klein of *Newsweek* wrote: "Flawed vehicle though he may be, Dan Quayle seems to have nudged presidential politics perilously close to something that really matters."[6] "Values talk" shaped a presidential campaign too often characterized by the now-you-see-him-now-you-don't tactics of Ross Perot, the difficulty of getting anything clear out of Bill Clinton, and the challenge of getting anything intelligent out of George Bush.

Family values were front and center.

With his "Ozzie and Harriet" antidote for the disturbing rise in America's urban violence and moral license, Dan Quayle kicked things off. But apparently, Americans are having a hard time living up to the Nelsons. Only one third of American families resemble the 1950s stereotype today. The divorce rate remains over fifty percent. Babies born to unmarried couples have tripled since 1970. Attending these trends are a sickening array of what the sociologists term "dysfunctions": an explosion in child abuse, crime, learning disabilities, and welfare dependency, to name only a few.

Changes in family structure alone haven't caused this

---

4. Joe Klein, "Whose Values?" *Newsweek* (June 8, 1992), p. 19.
5. Ibid.
6. Ibid.

mess. Economics plays a big role. In most two-parent families Harriet now has to work. Teenagers spend hours each week working in fast food chains and retail stores. Younger children are hustled off each morning for child care. Worry and hurry distance families emotionally and physically from one another.

And consider the issues Dan Quayle didn't talk about: the lure of success, the power of wealth, the greed and deceit of consumerism, the seduction of unchecked sexual passion. We live in a culture that celebrates buying rather than giving, possessing rather than belonging, conquering rather than serving. For millions of Americans, the thirst to enjoy the American Dream cannot be quenched. And it refuses to be controlled.

Concerned about these changes and anxious about the outcome of the 1992 Presidential election year, many groups rallied their constituents in order to push their particular agenda. The Christian Coalition, a conservative political watchdog, published its voter's guide rating America's politicians on their "family values" voting record.

But *whose* values? *Whose* morality? *Whose* family?

There is plenty of noise, but little agreement. America is in transition; traditions are overturned; rules are thrown by the wayside. In a Colorado restaurant, my eyes spotted a new kind of rhetoric. A waitress wore a button boldly asserting a new slogan: "Pro-child, Pro-family, Pro-choice." Double-take. Something didn't belong. I expected: "Pro-child, Pro-family, Pro-life." Another clue. The categories are getting blurred.

The Search for Identity

In the face of this disorienting transformation of American culture, the family gropes blindly for a new identity. For Dr. David Popenoe, Associate Dean for the Social Sciences at Rutgers University, the data lead to an unmistakable conclu-

9

sion: we are witnessing the breakup of the American family as we know it.

> . . . during the past 25 years, family decline in the U.S., as in other industrialized societies, has been both steeper and more alarming than during any other quarter century in history. Although they may not use the term decline, most scholars now agree — though for many this represents a recent change of viewpoint — that the family has undergone a social transformation during this period. Some see "dramatic and unparalleled changes," while others call it a "veritable revolution."[7]

Popenoe identifies two remedies, but proposes a third. One possible remedy is a return to the structure of the traditional nuclear family, popularized by Ozzie and Harriet Nelson, and affirmed by Dan Quayle. The family looks something like this: two parents, wife at home, husband comes home from work to a pair of smiling freckled kids playing ball in the yard, while dinner cooks in the oven.

Less romantic, and possibly more dangerous, the second remedy requires the active and extensive involvement of the federal government to develop policies and create structures enhancing family life. The current liberal democratic administration is in many ways trying to do this. Family becomes a program of American politics. But *whose* values, *whose* family, *whose* understanding of the truth sets the standard?

Popenoe is rightly dissatisfied with these two remedies. Instead, he suggests the need for a whole new social movement whose purpose is to promote families and their values within the new constraints of modern life. We cannot return to some shimmering image of nuclear bliss from the past, nor can we

---

7. David Popenoe, "The Breakup of the Family: Can We Reverse the Trend?" *USA Today* (May 1991), pp. 50-53.

allow government to dictate what family is going to be and how it is going to exist.

In our society, many groups aspire to the role of defining and promoting "family": liberal, conservative, straight, and gay. Popenoe himself never identifies any movement; he simply identifies the need: Where is that movement of people who will demonstrate family to us?

I wonder if the church of Jesus Christ is listening.

Movements are a dime a dozen. They start at the drop of a hat. They end just as quickly. Movements attract followers quickly. Some are better at it than others. The trouble with a movement is that it typically has few, if any, membership requirements. A person doesn't necessarily have to believe its ideals, and may not have to live by them. Many of those who attach themselves to such movements are like empty bottles tossed into a river: they are simply carried along by the current.

Frankly, more than a mere movement is needed. What America (and the world) needs is the church. The church is that peculiar community sent into this world with a peculiar task: live and tell the good news of Jesus Christ. Among other things, the church must be a place where the gospel of Jesus Christ is made believable in the face of unbelief by a group of men, women, and children who believe it and live by it. The church must also be a place where people can be real with one another, find guidance for living with the pain of irreconcilable differences, and see models of healthy relationships. In a world like ours the local church may be the only place many of us can go to experience "family."

By virtue of our baptism into God's new family, anyone, regardless of race, gender, ability, or income can enjoy "insider" status. Baptized into Christ's death and resurrection, we belong. The church of Jesus Christ, and the message we proclaim, is God's answer to our predicament. The church is that commu-

11

nity of people sent by God to demonstrate family life to a culture groping blindly for answers.

Here's the bottom line: Americans will learn to become families only by learning to become the church. The church's witness to God's design for human life together is based upon the seemingly arrogant claim that we have seen God act and heard God speak in ways others haven't. Our witness is grounded in the conviction that without repentance, and con-version — *a new birth* — all human life is lived in real rebellion against God.

That doesn't go over too well on Main Street today. In my community, there was a time when Main Street was jammed with traffic on Sunday mornings as people commuted back and forth to church. Today, Main Street is fairly quiet. The oc-casional church visitor has little problem finding a parking place in local church parking lots. Instead, traffic is backed up at the entrance to the large shopping mall, and parking is hard to find at popular restaurants. The church address may still be the same, but the street itself has changed irrevocably.

CHAPTER 2

A Sign of the Times

THE NEW sign hung triumphantly on the shopkeeper's door: "Open on Sundays." New owners, new pastries, and new ideas combined to draw shoppers to an old bakery. Was the new sign a flash-in-the-pan marketing gimmick, or a sign of the times? No one knew for sure.

Across the street and down a few shops, Frances and her husband Lou faced a dilemma. They owned and operated a clothing store established years ago by her father. Since their reputation was firmly established in the valley, the store faced no real competition. Business was good, customers loyal, and profits consistent. But the bakery presented a fresh opportunity. The bakery proved that many shoppers didn't hesitate to stop for a few items after church on Sunday. These were the 1960s. Times were changing. If customers wanted to shop on Sundays, maybe it was time to open the doors.

"Sam says the hardware store's thinking of opening at noon on Sundays," Lou mused after Saturday's last customer left the store. He shut the door and turned the sign. "Sam says there's money to be made."

"I know," replied Frances. "But daddy made a commitment . . ."

"And we made a promise," said Lou. They'd covered this ground before.

"Lou, it won't last. Never does when people break God's rules."

For years Lou and Frances wrestled with the pressure. Each time they bravely determined to follow her father's commitment: the store would always close on Sunday, in honor of the Sabbath.

Last week I drove past Frances' and Lou's clothing store. A new sign hung in the window: "For Sale." The sign, together with the empty storefronts along this once busy downtown street, marks the end of an age. The new sign in the baker's window thirty years ago was not a flash-in-the-pan marketing gimmick. It signaled something much deeper: the death of one era, and the birth of another.

The Collapse of Christendom

For many American families, Sunday shopping is a tradition. Few retailers refuse to open on Sundays; few Americans refuse to shop. In many parts of the country, Sunday is the busiest and most profitable shopping day of the week. But it was not always that way.

Older Americans remember the days when all labor and commercial activities were forbidden on Sundays — by law. The Blue Laws, or Sunday closing laws, forced Americans to observe Sunday as a day of rest in deference to the Ten Commandments. The fourth of these commandments charged Israel to observe the Sabbath as a holy day of rest (Exodus 20:8; Deuteronomy 5:12). With its roots firmly grounded in the Old Testament as well as the New, the Christian church has generally observed the Sabbath as well.

For several hundred years, American civilization was generally structured around a common religious view of life drawn from the Bible. In most American villages, towns, and cities, the Christian church, often represented in all its denominational diversity, was the center of the community. The definition and practice of American family life was forged from the Judeo-Christian heritage. For most, Sunday was a symbol of these dominant American values: church and family.

Today, though Sunday is still part of America's vocabulary, Sabbath is not. For some who recognize the word it brings to mind images of better days — full churches, big Sunday dinners, quiet Sunday afternoons. But for others, the word brings to mind images of Puritanical religion, legalism, and tradition — things long out of fashion. Both images are alive in our churches today. The church I serve is no exception.

Covenant Church has worked hard to build a Sunday School program that fashions modern Christians who can live faithfully in a world that often makes faithfulness to Jesus Christ intensely difficult. So have many churches. We think we've done a pretty good job. But at a recent Christian Education Committee meeting we were forced to stare at our declining attendance figures. Our curriculum is solid, our teachers outstanding, but our people are not coming. Everyone had a reason.

An older member of the committee said that we lack commitment. "We need a good sermon on commitment to Sunday School," she said; "the kind Dr. Lawrence used to preach!"

The group was silent.

"We could have an attendance contest," another suggested. "It worked a few years ago. People really responded to the challenge."

"Those things don't go over well with my group," interjected a woman in her early forties. "Our kids have games here, lessons there. Husbands and wives and kids all work. It's chaos. We're fragmented and frayed. There's no time to be together!" She was getting emotional — that makes Presbyterians nervous. "We're *stressed* out! Sunday mornings are the only time many families have together." The room fell silent again. "I'm not saying it's *right.* I'm just telling you the way it *is.*"

Now we were getting somewhere. Sitting there that night, we began to feel the enormity of the situation: a crisis faces many American families and churches. Today's families are broken. We are separated geographically and emotionally. Many ache in loneliness and despair. People feel like outsiders in their own families.

And the church? It seems apathetic, lethargic, impotent. Many Americans say "Yes" to God, but "No" to the church. Belonging to a local church is no longer important. Churches, once the center of our communities, and the Bible, once foundational to American civilization, are being pushed to the periphery. Attendance at church plays second fiddle to weekend outings, athletic events, sleeping in. We are a society of joiners. Church is just one more obligation on a long list of obligations.

America is simply not the place it used to be. Church and family, institutions long central to American culture, are crumbling before our eyes.

As we sat and talked and listened, we began to recognize that both the family and the church face the same problem. We find ourselves living in a culture we do not recognize. It doesn't share our values, nor does it worship our God. It couldn't care less about our traditions.

We're not sure how or when it happened, or how we could have been so blind. But we are sure that for too long most of the church has been seduced by a dangerous lie. Both liberals and conservatives have assumed that American culture is basically Christian, that it needs no real conversion. Just a little more moralism, a few more decisions for Christ, an extra helping of social action will pull things in line. No. Most Americans have accommodated the gospel of the Kingdom of God to a civil religion that identifies Jesus Christ with our religious, social, and political agendas — whether liberal or conservative. We have packaged our odd God and made the gospel, our churches, and our families socially acceptable. In doing so, we seem to have lost the essence of New Testament discipleship.

We face a crisis. The problem is not superficial; neither is the solution. Tinkering with curriculum and teachers is child's play. Attendance contests and canned evangelism programs are gimmicks. Pulpit antics are merely Band-Aids.

Our church's Christian Education Committee was sent back to school for a few lessons in history. Many of us knew that during its first three hundred years, conversion to Christianity was generally a dangerous move. At best, Christians were merely tolerated by the Roman government and populace. At worst, they were persecuted and martyred. Few of us knew how and why that changed.

Early in the fourth century, the Roman Emperor, Constantine, declared Christianity the official religion of the Roman Empire. Christendom was born. For over sixteen centuries, western civilization has been dominated by essentially the same worldview. Our assumptions, values, and ideals have generally come from the Judeo-Christian tradition. If people were not necessarily on the same page, they were basically reading from the same Book. Some measure of uniformity helps to hold an empire together. Though we have had our problems, things have worked fairly well within this kind of environment.

But today, the bulk of Americans no longer read from the same Book. This is merely stating the obvious. Not so obvious are the implications. Careful observers tell us that we are witnessing an unprecedented transformation of American culture. Christendom, the thick chord that once held western European and American culture together, has frayed and snapped. Put another

17

way, the particular perception of truth and ethics that served as the foundation for western civilization for more than 1600 years has finally collapsed. America no longer finds it necessary to uphold the values of the Christian church. Many Americans have grown bold enough to stop pretending they ever did. This backdrop better helps us understand the changes in American culture generally. It also helps us make better sense of Jerrold Footlick's specific words regarding the American family:

> The American family does not exist. Rather, we are creating many American families, of diverse styles and shapes. In unprecedented numbers, our families are unalike: we have fathers working while mothers keep house; fathers and mothers both working away from home; single parents; second marriages bringing children together from unrelated backgrounds; childless couples; unmarried couples, with and without children; gay and lesbian parents. We are living through a period of historic change in American family life.[1]

Another sign of the times. Constantine's project is finished; a new one has begun. The quicker we come to recognize the fact, the better off our churches and families will be.

What is the shape of this emerging American culture? Two trends are important for our purpose. First, the privatization of religion to the realm of individual values and opinions. And second, the rise of spiritual pluralism.

The Privatization of Religion

When our ancestors settled America, they considered it a holy experiment. The early colonists viewed their mission as God-

---

1. Jerrold K. Footlick, "What Happened to the Family?" *Newsweek*, Special Issue (Winter/Spring, 1990), p. 15.

given. They were on an errand into the wilderness, destined to build a city on a hill. In 1630, Governor John Winthrop of the Massachusetts Bay Company spoke these words while sailing for New England: "We shall find that the God of Israel is among us. . . . we shall be as a city upon a hill, the eyes of all people are upon us."[2]

It was an important experiment. From this vision, and others similar to it, grew an impressive and influential modern civilization. Fleeing the religious totalitarianism of England and Europe, the colonists set out to build a holy commonwealth demonstrating religious tolerance: Congregationalists, Anglicans, Presbyterians, Quakers, Baptists, and Jews all found a home. From the beginning the experiment was marked by occasional failures in tolerance — some quite ugly. Our Founders quarreled regularly over the various ways they read the same Book, and how they would exercise their interpretations politically. The experiment eventually led to the Bill of Rights and the First Amendment, which guaranteed religious liberty. The separation of church and state became a doctrine central to the American enterprise.

I've watched this doctrine in action here in my own community. On January 5, 1994, a publicly elected official suggested that the weekly meetings of the Mercer County commissioners open with a word of prayer. "Why should we not acknowledge our need for divine guidance when all around us cry for spiritual help and guidance?" the commissioner asked. He argued that commissioners should model those values and practices held dear to those they are elected to represent. The suggestion erupted in strong debate throughout the community.

The editor of the *Sharon Herald* newspaper (January 13, 1994) wrote to set things straight. By reminding readers of the

2. Sydney E. Ahlstrom, A *Religious History of the American People* (New Haven and London: Yale University Press, 1972), p. 147.

Supreme Court's ban on prayer in public school early in the 1960s, the editor argued that the real issue is not a question of the value of prayer and religion. Rather, the issue hinges on the practice of religion in a pluralistic community where people don't necessarily hold the same beliefs and values. "Any prayer offered in commissioners' meetings could offend by preferring one religion over another," warned the editor. This isn't to say that commissioners shouldn't pray when a meeting begins, only that anyone acting in public ought to "pray in secret — to himself — and not inflict his beliefs on anyone who may not agree with them."

The editor's advice? Public officials must keep religion out of politics in order to avoid offending those who don't share their views. "Let them pray," he says in closing, but let them pray "silently."

This is not only a local issue. A letter to the editor of the *Wall Street Journal* illustrated the same sentiment. Arthur Kropp is President of *People for the American Way* — a liberal political watchdog. His letter was a spirited defense of Constitutional liberty; both Kropp and his organization are dead set on ensuring that the political arena is kept free of that messy business of religious belief. In his letter, he argued that "the vast majority of Americans vote their political interests, not their religious beliefs." Candidates should be judged on whether or not their views are acceptable to voters, not on their religious convictions. Period. Unfortunately, Kropp laments, there remain some who stubbornly "judge candidates based on where they worship rather than where they stand."[3] And that offends him. Deeply.

The message is clear: whether you're a candidate or a voter, by all means practice religion if you want to, but do it *silently*.

---

3. Arthur J. Kropp, "'Unfair' Charges of Religious Bigotry," *People for the American Way* (Washington, D.C., January 1994), p. 4.

Anything more is offensive. And we must not risk offending anyone!

The gospel, that announcement which rocked the temples and palaces and marketplaces of the ancient world with the offensive claim that "Jesus Christ is Lord!" cannot even be whispered in public today. The news of God's judgment and salvation proclaimed in the life, death, and resurrection of Jesus Christ is relegated to the status of private values and opinions; it is dismissed as having no claim on the public world of so-called "facts." Tamed, domesticated, and neutered, the Lion of Judah has become nothing more than a common family house cat.

The Rise of Spiritual Pluralism

Those early American political ideals, tolerance and religious plurality, find their fullest expression in contemporary America. The privatization of religious devotion in America leads to a type of pluralism probably never envisioned by our Founders. The Judeo-Christian worldview no longer dominates the American scene. No longer are our lives shaped by the Puritan vision of a world defined by biblical revelation.

Instead, the Enlightenment project of the seventeenth and eighteenth centuries promises to jettison an obsolete religious vision and replace it with a modern one. Human reason, not divine revelation, must dictate the definition of society. The future of this planet is not in God's hands but in ours. This popular sentiment is well articulated in the Humanist Manifesto II: "humans are responsible for what we are or will become. No deity will save us; we must save ourselves."[4]

---

4. Humanist Manifesto II, published in the September/October 1973 issue of *The Humanist*, by the American Humanist Association (Amherst, New York).

But not all Americans are content with this modern, secular vision. Some, as dissatisfied with the modern "no God" vision of the universe as with the traditional "one God" vision of creation, are now exploring a postmodern spirituality of Mother Earth. In his article "Planet Water: The Spirituality of H2O," Kirkpatrick Sale laments the so-called "secularization" of water, and attacks monotheism in general and the Judeo-Christian tradition in particular as the culprit. By observing modern Christians, Jews, and Muslims, Sale concludes that water is regarded by them as "only one more element to be manipulated at the whim of the one true God."[5] (Given the church's dismal failure to tend creation in the name of God, Sale's indictment is understandable. But given the Bible's teaching on the value of God's creation, his conclusion couldn't be more misguided.) According to Sale, traditional western religion views both water and earth as resources to be exploited. As such, western religion is not only outdated, he argues, it is *dangerous*.

But traditional monotheistic religion isn't Sale's only target. Science, that discipline birthed by the Judeo-Christian and Muslim worldviews, eventually wrenched water from its good and sacred place as the source of life itself; water was reduced to "exactly two molecules of one element, one of another, and became simply a happenstance, a fortuitous combination of atoms."[6]

Traditional religion and traditional science . . . both are enemies of this flowering new age.

What do Sale and many others propose? True enlightenment comes when we cast off the shackles of traditional religion and science. We must rediscover what the ancients knew before

5. Kirkpatrick Sale, "Planet Water: The Spirituality of H2O," *Utne Reader* (May/June 1993), p. 76.
6. Ibid.

the world was infected by the arrogance of Jewish, Christian, and Islamic monotheism, and the materialism of the scientific age. He says that most previous cultures recognized water as divine. He tells us that *Sulis* was the ancient Celtic goddess of water. The Aztecs worshipped *Chal-chi-uhtl-icue.* Water was the goddess *Sisi-utl* for Indians along California's coast. Persian myth celebrated *Analinda* as the goddess of water, and the Babylonians worshipped *Apsu* and *Tiamat.* In this new age, we too, Sale argues, must recognize not only water, but the whole earth as divine.[7]

The new, post-Christian project reveals that America is not so much becoming secular as it is turning to neopaganism. Our nation has become a veritable marketplace of ideas and gods, bought and sold in response to American consumer appetites.

A Sense of Mission

As Christians, we should expect pluralism. It is the context of Christian mission. The gospel enters a world flooded with religion, brimming with idolatry. This is the fertile soil of Christian proclamation. Into this kind of world we speak the hope of the gospel. Taking Jesus at his word, we must expect and celebrate repentance (Acts 18:9-10), and we must also expect and endure rejection (Luke 10:10-12). But the experience of rejection must never silence us. We are commissioned to speak. The nature of the church, and the families that make up the church, is grounded in the person and work of Jesus Christ, who gives us a mission: "As the Father sent me, so I am sending you" (John 20:21); he also gives us a promise: "You shall be my witnesses" (Acts 1:8).

7. Ibid.

23

In Japanese, the character for "crisis" is a combination of the characters for "danger" and "opportunity" (or "promise").[8] Every crisis opens the door for a fresh beginning. Here in this fear-filled, anxious place both danger and opportunity meet. The future hangs in a balance; events can go either way. Luke makes this clear in his Gospel, but especially in the Acts of the Apostles. Every crisis for the early church provided a fresh opportunity for witness, but each crisis also exposed the church to danger.

Talking, listening, thinking, and praying, our church's Christian Education Committee gradually recognized that the problems of the family and the problems of the church were related. That may be obvious, but our group saw the connection in a new way. We face a crisis, and it is monumental. But we are God's church, and God turned the horror of Good Friday's Cross into the wonder and hope of Easter's Empty Tomb. The present crisis creates a fresh opportunity for the church to reassert its rightful place as a witness to the truth and power of God.

An ordinary administrative church committee embraced a profound sense of mission. We were transformed. We learned that we are not simply managing a religious institution; we are commissioned to build a church capable of authentic witness to God's design for all human life, including our families. A church faithful to Jesus Christ will not bemoan the problems of society; instead it will give birth to individuals and families whose conversion makes them genuine signs of the Kingdom wherever God sends them.

For some, the present crisis is a devastating blow; it means the end of America as we know it. But for others it is a gift from God — *a wake-up call*. It is exhilarating. It may be danger-

8. David J. Bosch, *Transforming Mission: Paradigm Shifts in Theology of Mission* (Maryknoll, New York: Orbis Books, 1991), p. 3.

ous. The way forward is neither a liberal sellout to the sweeping cultural changes, nor a conservative retreat to the American ideals of yesterday. The way forward must be truly evangelical and prophetic. We must hear God speak:

> Do not remember the former things,
>   or consider the things of old.
> I am about to do a new thing;
>   now it springs forth, do you not perceive it?
> I will make a way in the wilderness
>   and rivers in the desert.   (Isaiah 43:18, 19)

In this crisis God summons the church — the individuals and families joined together by faith — to reclaim their missionary identity. To that task we must now turn.

PART II

THE FAMILY RECOVERS ITS IDENTITY

CHAPTER 3

Exile: Strangers in the Land

FACING change is nothing new for God's people. Change comes with the calling: Abraham's holy adventure, Israel's bondage in Egypt, Israel's conquest of Canaan, Israel's exile in Babylon, the church's scattering throughout the Mediterranean world. Every change presented a new threat and a new opportunity to the people of God — culturally, politically, religiously.

Change is central to both the church's message and its vocation. The Bible's drama moves from the Garden of Eden to the City of God — the New Jerusalem of John's Revelation. It is a *pilgrimage*. That's important. God's people are pilgrims, not vagabonds. A vagabond is a tramp, wandering undirected except by a gnawing internal restlessness — the proverbial wanderlust.

A pilgrim, though often restless, is guided by a profound sense of purpose. Pilgrims are people on a mission, and a pilgrim's mission means more than a change of address. It means more than packing belongings, loading camels, dealing with meddling in-laws, tending tired children, listening to homesick spouses. It means that in the process of following God, the pilgrim people are changed — *transformed*.

LETTERS TO A CHURCH IN CRISIS

Communication is critical in times of crisis. Most of the Bible's many authors wrote with the purpose of communicating a message from God regarding particular problems faced by believers. Two letters in particular were addressed to communities facing circumstances not altogether different from our own: the first from a prophet, the second a pastor. These letters are especially potent when we allow ourselves to listen to the ways they confront and challenge the lives of those who first heard them.

Life in a Dazzling New Home

In 597 B.C.E. Nebuchadnezzar's army marched against Jerusalem and sacked it. Destroying the Temple, razing virtually all the fortified towns in Judah, and deporting the nation's political, intellectual, and religious leadership to Babylon, Nebuchadnezzar presented Israel with its most dangerous crisis. Thousands died in battle. Thousands died of starvation and disease. Thousands more fled for their lives. Who knows how many were executed? Those left in the land were a demoralized and despondent remnant. They were forced to rebuild their lives in full view of the wreckage: the Temple, palace, and city walls lay in ruins.

From the wreckage, the prophet Jeremiah wrote a letter to those marched in chains across the hot sands to a new home far away.

> These are the words that the prophet Jeremiah sent from Jerusalem to the remaining elders among the exiles, and to the priests, the prophets, and all the people, whom Nebuchadnezzar had taken into exile from Jerusalem to Babylon. (Jeremiah 29:1)

Those deported to Babylon suffered the hardship and humiliation of foreign conquest and domination. Bombarded by physical, mental, and spiritual stresses, the exiled community longed for the familiar rocky hills of the Judean countryside. But as the darkness of culture shock lifted, the exiles awoke to find themselves in a dazzling new home.

The Babylonian policy toward prisoners of war was relatively benevolent. Rather than dispersing them among the Empire's population in order to break any remaining sense of national or ethnic loyalty, Babylon allowed conquered peoples to settle in internment camps. Though not liberated as full citizens, neither were they prisoners. They were free to build houses, farm their land, and engage in the commerce of Babylon.[1] They were allowed to rebuild their lives in full view of the splendor and power of the Empire.

Surrounded by a water moat sixty feet wide, Babylon's double wall provided a total defense depth of fifty-seven feet against invading armies. Nebuchadezzar's palace housed the Hanging Gardens of Babylon — a wonder of the ancient world.[2] The city itself was filled with temples celebrating more gods than Israel had ever heard of. The largest and most splendid of Babylon's temples was Esagila, home of the city's guardian god, Marduk. No one could gaze at its great ziggurat surrounded by fifty-five smaller chapels and walk its lavish processional street[3] and not be overwhelmed by Marduk's apparent superiority over all other gods, including the God of Israel whose Temple and city lay shattered by a Babylonian army.

All this had a purpose. The Babylonians recognized that

1. John Bright, A *History of Israel*, 3rd edn. (Philadelphia: Westminster Press, 1981), pp. 345-346.
2. D. J. Wiseman, "Babylon," *International Standard Bible Encyclopedia* (Grand Rapids: Eerdmans, 1979), 1.382ff.
3. S. H. Hook, *Babylonian and Assyrian Religion* (Norman: University of Oklahoma Press, 1963), pp. 43f.

pain, suffering, and oppression often galvanize rather than break a conquered people. They preferred Babylon to be viewed as a great benefactor, a host introducing a backward people to the wonders of modern civilization. Babylon's leadership knew the impression the great city and its religion would make on the leaders of this troublesome little nation called Israel.

The Babylonian Exile marks a decisive period in the life of the pilgrim people, Israel. The state was conquered. Israel's faith was shattered. Everything had changed: politics, culture, geography, religion. This new setting threatened the identity and destiny of the people of God. What kind of people would rise from the rubble? Much would depend on how the exiles received the prophet's letter.

Hundreds of years later, Jeremiah's letter provided a model for an aging pastor concerned to challenge the church to faithfulness in a new situation that threatened to make faithfulness intensely difficult.

Living between a Rock and a Hard Place

The death of Jesus dealt a crushing blow to the small band of his followers. In less than a week — from the delirious joy of Palm Sunday to the devastating horror of Good Friday — everything had changed. Their minds were dark, shut tight like the room in which they hid. Fear paralyzed them. Disoriented by the events of the past days, they dared not venture out. Then came the news: *"He is risen! We have seen him."*

Within a few decades, that first handful of disciples, changed by what they had seen and heard, carried the good news of the death and resurrection of Jesus Christ throughout the Mediterranean world. The mission led the church into crisis.

Initially viewed as a Jewish sect, early Christianity was implicitly awarded tolerance by the Roman Empire. The Jews were radical monotheists who tolerated no idolatry: "The LORD is our God, the LORD alone" (Deuteronomy 6:4). The Romans, on the other hand, worshipped a pantheon of gods, including various caesars. But lessons learned from the Exile and during the Maccabean period taught the Jews how to live safely in a potentially hostile setting. Prudently, the Jews had negotiated a religious détente with the Empire. As long as they kept to themselves, the Empire left them alone. It was a handy truce for both parties.

The early Christians were not quite so prudent. The movement was young and idealistic. Maybe they had not learned the fine art of compromise — the subtle loss of conviction, the seduction of truth. Maybe they really believed that the church's message is good news, public truth that must be told, a message that must not be compromised or domesticated regardless of the cost. The gospel is about salvation, personal and public, individual and global. Lesslie Newbigin urges that the gospel is the announcement of a fact, the declaration of the presence of the Kingdom, the reign of God. In a magazine like *Newsweek* this is not an interesting bit of journalism to be slotted somewhere between the "Sports" and "Drama" sections. It is front cover material.[4] The early Christians, as heralds of this news, were a political threat. They were unwilling to negotiate a truce or bend their convictions.

Both the Roman and Jewish authorities found the church arrogant, subversive, and dangerous. The welfare of the Roman Empire rested in part on the public's submission to or tolerance of Rome's civil religion: the worship of its gods and its Caesar. The Empire could not tolerate anyone who persisted in the

4. Lesslie Newbigin, *Mission in Christ's Way* (Geneva: WCC Publications, 1987), pp. 1-2.

claim that "Jesus is Lord" (1 Cor. 12:3) and refused to keep this conviction private.

Like the Romans, the Jewish leaders also recognized that political stability hinged upon faithfulness to common religious traditions. They would occasionally tolerate a religious heretic, but tolerance would not extend to this growing band of heretics who also jeopardized the political safety of Israel. The Christians caused problems, and the Jewish leaders feared Rome's reprisal. They were eager to set the record straight: the Jews made it clear that they wanted nothing to do with this Jesus or his followers.

Sometime during the last third of the first century, the small churches scattered throughout Asia Minor faced this crisis of mistrust and hostility. A pastor — Peter according to our tradition — knowing their trouble, sent a letter to guide and encourage them.

> Peter, an apostle of Jesus Christ. To the exiles of the Dispersion in Pontus, Galatia, Cappadocia, Asia, and Bithynia, who have been chosen and destined by God the Father and sanctified by the Spirit to be obedient to Jesus Christ and to be sprinkled with his blood: May grace and peace be yours in abundance. (1 Peter 1:1-2)

Are these Christians who gather in small house churches scattered throughout the villages and cities of ancient Turkey really exiles? No. This pastor uses an image rich with meaning to shape the identity of the church. Most of these Christians had not moved an inch. But they were converted, born again — *transformed*. That changed everything. Stepping out of the waters of baptism, they quickly found themselves in a world not at all happy about this change. In this new setting which threatened the identity and destiny of the people of God, what kind of people would endure the crisis? Much would depend on how the churches received the pastor's letter.

COPING WITH CHANGE

Change is always disorienting. And disorientation can be dangerous. A disoriented church can lose its soul if it does not know how to regain its bearings when it finds itself in unfamiliar territory. It takes more than a compass and a map: it takes faithfulness that can lead it safely past the twin dangers of escapism and assimilation.

Escapism

Like Washington Irving's "The Legend of Sleepy Hollow," the story of "Rip Van Winkle" lies tucked away in the forgotten catacombs of our brains. Most Americans read such stories as children. A large number can still rehearse portions of them. Most of us find little value in them today, except as outlandish entertainment for our children.

I don't know what Irving intended. Some Ph.D candidate has probably written a doctoral dissertation dissecting the social or political implications of Irving's tale. The author may have written with a larger purpose in mind. But whatever his intentions, "Rip Van Winkle" holds a powerful lesson.

The story opens with a problem: Rip is badly henpecked by his wife. It ends with a solution: Rip's nagging wife dies. Some children's story! The lesson in Irving's tale is not the warning that it's dangerous to nag, nor the encouragement to drink away life's problems. No, the story's power lies in the way it identifies the way most of us wish we could manage a nagging problem. In one sense, this isn't a children's story at all. It's an adult indictment couched cleverly as a children's tale. Irving wallops us before we know what he's doing.

As the drama unfolds we learn that Rip is so troubled by his wife that he is not at home in his own house. His only relief is his hunting. Out in the forest he forgets about his bitter life at home.

During one of his escapes into the forest, Rip meets a dwarfish creature. Intrigued, he and his dog follow the little man high into the "Kaatskill" mountains. The dwarf leads Rip to a mountain clearing where a number of these strange creatures play ninepins on the lawn; they drink large mugs of a strange brew. Thirsty, Rip helps himself, and promptly falls asleep.

On waking Rip fears he has slept through the night. "Oh," thinks Rip, "what excuse shall I make to Mrs. Van Winkle?" Disoriented, Rip stumbles home to his village.

> The village had changed since he saw it last. It was much larger. New houses had been built. Strange faces were at the windows. He thought this was the village he had left only the day before. There stood the Kaatskill Mountains. There ran the Hudson river. Rip was confused.
>
> Rip had trouble finding his own house. He listened to hear Mrs. Van Winkle scream at him. He found his house in bad condition. The roof had fallen in and the windows shattered. . . . Rip went into the house. No one was there.[5]

The Van Winkle address was still the same, but the house, the street, the town, the people had changed. Rip's bewilderment over his twenty-year nap quickly turned to euphoria when he discovered that his nagging wife had died during his absence!

The tale of Rip Van Winkle is more than a children's story. The tale illustrates the way many would like to cope with troublesome problems: *escapism*.

5. Washington Irving, *Rip Van Winkle and the Legend of Sleepy Hollow*, adapted by R. A. Pulliam and O. N. Darby (Austin: Steck-Vaughn Company, 1949), pp. 21-22.

Faced with the prophet Jeremiah's promise that they would spend seventy years in Babylonian captivity, many of the exiles were tempted to find a good bed, set the alarm, and sleep until the day they could return home to Jerusalem.

Finding themselves in an increasing difficult situation, the early Christians suffered the same temptation. Jesus promised to return; why not sleep until the rapture?

Escapism is common today. It has many forms. The reasons are legion. America is changing rapidly, and Christianity too often appears irrelevant and archaic. In most parts of our country the Christian church is no longer central to our community. It is a relic. Few Christians know how to cope. Many are tempted to drink from Rip's barrel.

Assimilation

But there is another way to cope with change. While many choose a bed, others jump in feet first and take a bath. Rather than escape, they immerse themselves in the intoxicating changes swirling around them.

By the time Cyrus, conqueror of the mighty Babylonian Empire, liberated the Jews and sent the first restoration party back to Jerusalem with the purpose of rebuilding the Temple, many Jews were firmly established in Babylonian culture. They had followed part of Jeremiah's counsel: "seek the welfare of the city where I have sent you into exile, and pray to the LORD on its behalf, for in its welfare you will find your welfare" (Jeremiah 29:7). A large number were wealthy. According to the ancient Jewish historian Josephus, they were "not willing to leave their possessions."[6]

In addition to accumulating wealth, many Jews achieved

6. Josephus, *Antiquities of the Jews* 11.1.3, quoted in Bright, p. 363.

religious enlightenment while in Babylon. The rigid, exclusive, intolerant traditions of their ancestors were reshaped by the encounter with the religious pluralism of Babylonian civilization. The God of the Hebrews was just one among many — another culture's expression of a universal religious quest.

These factors influenced a large number of Jews who were so well assimilated into Babylonian culture that when the call came to return, it was no longer a call to return home; home lay in Babylon, not Judea.

The same story can be told of Rome in the first century and America in the twentieth — whenever the church succumbs to the seductions of the Empire and loses a sense of its true home. Social scientist George Barna provides a powerful metaphor to describe the temptation and the danger.

He tells us that if we place a frog in a kettle of room temperature water, it won't fuss. It sits content in its comfortable little world. Gradually increasing the temperature of the water, we find that the frog continues to enjoy its bath. Apparently unaware of its changing environment (perhaps unconcerned), the frog fails to recognize the dangerous change. It cooks in the boiling water.[7]

If the church remains complacent about the changes in our environment we face a grave danger. We're not in danger of death; the church and its mission is God's promise, not our program. Our failure will not thwart God's purpose. However, our ignorance and apathy will render us faithless and disobedient. The church in America is in danger on at least two fronts.

First, it is in danger of becoming so much like the culture that we can no longer speak the message of the gospel — a word of hope and of judgment. The current emphasis on making the

7. George Barna, *The Frog in the Kettle* (Ventura: Regal Books, 1990), p. 21.

gospel "relevant" is such a seduction. Many American churches build preaching, teaching, and program around the "felt needs" of our congregations and those we want to reach. We want the gospel to make real contact with real people where they live and work each day. This is a worthy project.

But the project becomes twisted when we too easily narrow the gap between an often embarrassingly strange biblical world and our more "civilized" modern world. We tame the gospel. Repackage our odd God. Make God, gospel, and Kingdom palatable to consumer appetites.

Second, if the church is virtually indistinguishable from the prevailing culture, the very people searching for the gospel won't hear it. Most Americans have had enough exposure to the Christian message to be effectively inoculated against it. Many Americans no longer *want* to listen to us.

Modern western culture is coming apart at the seams. The church is not faring much better. Crime, racism, disease, poverty, unemployment threaten the American dream. People are searching for hope, a way out. In America, the Christian message is often so closely identified with a dying culture that people assume Jesus is the problem, not the answer. And when Christians are virtually indistinguishable from anyone else, our message has little integrity.

Is it any wonder that the church appears impotent to address the changing culture of North America with gospel truth? When the church chooses either a bed or a bath it entertains disobedience; when we slumber like Rip Van Winkle or indulge in comfortable but fatal conformity to the culture, we become a curse rather than a blessing. Neither way is the way of Jesus Christ and the church in the world.

There is another way.

Exiles

The churches who received Peter's letter were sent to announce the gospel of Jesus Christ to their world, news that demanded the conversion of the Roman Empire. The Empire, for its part, threatened to convert the church. Mighty Rome appeared invincible and unrepentant.

Imperial powers quickly grow intolerant of the church when Christians refuse to worship at their altars — whether of Roman gods or the modern American trinity of money, sex, and power. Those who confess Jesus as Lord are implicated with One executed for treason and heresy. We are guilty by association. Like the Christians who received Peter's letter, many of us feel disoriented, threatened, afraid.

"Having a hard time, are you?" says Peter.

"Suffering . . . persecution . . . doubt. Feel like you don't belong? Wonder about this salvation business?" he continues. Like any good preacher, Peter grabs for an analogy, a metaphor to help them understand.

"What's it like?" he says. "It's like you're an alien residing in a foreign country."

Silence. Blank stares. The illustration doesn't connect with the audience.

"Wait," he continues. "It's like you're exile."

An old man leans forward slightly. A young mother lifts her eyes from her nursing child.

"Remember the exiles?"

"We remember."

"But what does that have to do with us?" another asks. "Most of us live in the city where we were born. Our families live in homes where our parents lived. A few of us are slaves, but there's not an exile among us!"

"Were you baptized?" asks Peter.

"Of course."

"When you were baptized, you *moved*," presses Peter. "The waters of baptism are a drowning, a relocating, a rebirth. In baptism you are given a new identity. You are adopted, born again into God's new society, the church. You serve a different ruler. You live by different rules. You become an *exile*."

Connection. The audience is all ears.

"You are a chosen race, a royal priesthood, a holy nation, God's own people, in order that you may proclaim the mighty acts of him who called you out of darkness into his marvelous light." Preaching now, Peter recalls the words of the prophet Hosea, "Once you were not a people, but now you are God's people; once you had not received mercy, but now you have received mercy" (1 Peter 2:9, 10).

What does this have to do with the American family? The crisis facing the family in America is a symptom of an even larger crisis: a pervasive loss of identity and mission in the church. Recovery will not come by tinkering with social policy, redefining the nature of the family, or communicating twelve steps for wholeness. What we need is *the church* — that peculiar community sent into this world with a peculiar task: live and tell the good news of Jesus Christ. We need the church to demonstrate visibly and persuasively what it means to be the family — *God's Family* of families living under God's rule.

We need to begin talking not about families per se or American families, but about *church families*. We need *church families* who refuse to fall asleep, *church families* who resist the temptation to disengage from the role given in baptism, *church families* who refuse to be identified as part of the fabric of the surrounding culture — just one thread among many. We need *transformed* church families who practice the exilic lifestyle inaugurated by baptism. Says Walter Brueggemann, "Exile is a sense of not belonging, of being in an environment hostile to the values of this community and its vocation. Exile is practiced

41

among those who refuse to accept and be assimilated into the new situation."[8]

Many Christians increasingly experience the sensation of being outsiders. We're made to feel like we don't quite fit in, we don't belong. We're made to feel wrong or intolerant or old fashioned or small-minded. Of course we don't belong! The church is most at home when it doesn't belong. We follow this man from Nazareth — Jesus Christ. This fool who died on the cross. This intensely odd God.

Many of us are tempted to fit in, bend our God-given convictions, convince ourselves that God cannot really mean for us to feel lonely, rejected, ignored, foolish. Who among us will remember that we were baptized into the name of Jesus Christ? He who was treated as an outsider, a traitor, a heretic, a fool, calls us to follow him.

8. Walter Brueggemann, "An Evangelical Rereading of Communal Experience," *Reading and Preaching the Book of Isaiah*, ed. Christopher R. Seitz (Philadelphia: Fortress Press, 1988), p. 88.

CHAPTER 4

Babylon: Naming the Powers

IN THE mid-1980s my wife Julie and I moved to Los Angeles from Denver, Colorado. The move marked a major transition in our lives, the opening of a new chapter. Adventure called us. We set out boldly, knowing no one. The only part of Los Angeles Julie had ever seen was the inside of the airport. My experience was limited to a brief business trip a year earlier.

Several days and twelve hundred miles later, excitement invigorated our road-weary bodies as we descended from the high desert into the Los Angeles basin. The end of the road was nearly in sight.

Driving along the 210 Freeway, we began to acquaint ourselves with the sights and sounds of new surroundings: street names, stores, signs, trees and plants and flowers — our senses were bombarded. Everything from the license plates to the geography was new.

"There, off to the right, are the San Gabriel mountains," I told Julie. "They soar up from the valley floor, over a mile high."

We both craned our necks for a look.

"Where?"

Our first lesson. Coastal fog, mixed with Los Angeles smog,

would often hide the most common landmarks from our sight. We would have to learn other ways to keep our bearings in this foreign city.

Setting up utilities was frustrating, opening bank accounts time-consuming, grocery shopping exhausting. We asked questions about everything. The sights, sounds, smells, faces were all unfamiliar. We found our new surroundings both exciting and intimidating.

But it didn't take long to adjust. We lived near the corner of Madison and Walnut, in a city named Pasadena. We bought groceries at Ralph's, and worked on Colorado Boulevard. Mike and Alice, Carl, Rupali, Cheryl, Jamie and Anne, all became close friends. We traveled the Pasadena Freeway, played at Manhattan Beach, walked at the Rose Bowl.

Learning the names of people, places, and things helped us learn the lay of the land. Naming our surroundings helped us keep our bearings in our new home.

Voices from Exile: From Palace to Patmos

Members of God's new family know what it means to live as pilgrims, exiles, strangers in a strange land. They need a way to recover and maintain their bearings when familiar landmarks disappear. Learning names can be an act of reconnaissance.

Daniel and Revelation model just such a capacity for naming, for identifying the hostile landscape in which we find ourselves. But these biblical books typically suffer from either misuse or neglect, much to our detriment. The time is ripe for rediscovery.

The prophecies and visions of both Daniel and Revelation orient a disoriented church to God and gospel and Kingdom. By naming those powers resistant and often hostile to gospel and church, they teach us to remain poised in the midst of crisis. They enable us to resist faithlessness and fear. Both prophetic works call the church to reclaim an exilic lifestyle by naming the powers of the surrounding cultures. Both prophets name the powers "Babylon."

Four Courageous Israelites in Nebuchadnezzar's Palace

The book of Daniel begins by narrating a story: the siege and defeat of Jerusalem by Nebuchadnezzar's armies. This defeat utterly devastated Judah. We cannot underestimate the crisis of faith God's people endured. This was not merely a political, economic, social defeat. It was this and more. It was theological and spiritual. Not only was a nation conquered; apparently so was its God.

Less a contest of military strength, stamina, or strategy, this was seen as a titanic duel of the gods. Nebuchadnezzar was not content to conquer Jerusalem and deport Israel's leadership to exile in Babylon; his armies desecrated the Temple, looting the courts, altar, and sanctuary. The vessels used in Temple worship were the closest thing Israel had to the idolatrous images of the pagans. These vessels were Nebuchadnezzar's real prize. Here was irrefutable evidence: Babylon's king and his god ruled supreme over Israel's king and his God.[1]

In Babylon, the vessels were placed in the conqueror's treasury of the gods — a gallery displaying the military and religious superiority of Babylon over all other nations and gods. The authority of Israel's worldview was not only questioned, it was replaced. Israel's great confession of faith, "Hear, O Israel: The LORD is our God, the LORD alone" (Deuteronomy 6:4), was ridiculed. And, given the evidence, who could argue?

1. John E. Goldingay, *Daniel*, The Word Biblical Commentary (Dallas: Word Books, 1989), p. 15.

From the outset, the narrator wants to set the record straight. The God of Israel *allowed* Judah to fall into Nebuchadnezzar's power, he says. The Lord of Hosts *allowed* Nebuchadnezzar to carry the holy vessels from the Temple and toss them into the gallery of his gods. He urges his readers not to be deceived by appearances, or intimidated by Babylon's arrogance: the God of Israel is still in charge.

The Empire was powerful, its leadership shrewd. Dominating powers wish to make conversion as swift and sure as possible. Nebuchadnezzar moved quickly to insure the absolute loyalty of Israel — this strange people who worshipped such an odd God. With Israel's holy vessels neatly decorating the king's gallery, Nebuchadnezzar now sought smart, handsome, and loyal Jews to decorate his palace.

The King ordered his palace executive, Ashpenaz, to recruit and train a handful of young Israelite nobility for service in the palace. They were the cream of the crop, those best able to absorb the finest liberal arts education available anywhere. They weren't merely given a scholarship, they were wined and dined, given royal treatment. After three years they were ready to fulfill their role as servants of the state.[2]

The narrator tells us that among this group were Daniel, Hananiah, Mishael, and Azariah, from the tribe of Judah. Since sectarian names were considered subversive and inappropriate, the Babylonians gave them new names: Daniel they called Belteshazzar, Hananiah they called Shadrach, Mishael they called Meshach, and Azariah they called Abednego.

By re-educating and renaming these Jewish leaders, the Empire intended to talk them out of Jewish perceptions of reality and into Babylonian definitions of reality. The Babylonian program intended to purge the exiles of their loyalty to an old and backward way of life defined by the Law of Moses,

2. Ibid., p. 17.

and to define life in terms of Babylonian religion and politics instead.[3] (I don't think the Babylonian program was too different from the agenda of our modern liberal democracy, best expressed by the programs of most of our higher educational institutions.) From Babylon's perspective there was nothing sinister about the program. It was altruistic, generous. They were bringing light to eyes long darkened by superstition and ignorance.

Conflict was inevitable. The story tells us that our four heroes finished their education and were providentially given positions of significant political power. Then in a burst of political genius, Nebuchadnezzar devised a plan to demonstrate the solidarity of his Empire. He crafted a magnificent golden statue that symbolized the ultimate fusion of Babylonian religion and politics. He orchestrated a service of dedication that summoned participants to worship before his statue. Finally, he demanded total compliance. Nonparticipation in the imperial worship ceremony implied nonconformity to the values of the Empire. It meant death in Babylon's fiery furnace.

This is not an isolated case. Empires often exploit the religious impulses of their people. Kings, presidents, and other state officials often bend their knees to God not as genuine expressions of worship but in order to enlist God and the religious in their political causes. No leadership, even church leadership, is exempt from civil religion. In 1933, German church leader Emmanuel Hirsch found himself spellbound by Adolf Hitler, and believed him to be a heaven-sent Christian politician. He was certain that no other people in the world enjoyed a leader "who takes Christianity so seriously." Hirsch continued, "On 1 May when Adolf Hitler closed his great speech with a prayer, the whole world could sense the wonderful

---

3. Cf. Walter Brueggemann, *Hopeful Imagination: Prophetic Voices in Exile* (Philadelphia: Fortress Press, 1986), ch. 5.

sincerity in that [act]."[4] Too many Christians in our century have been unable to resist conformity to state-imposed sanctions. We have too rarely recognized "Babylon" and its idolatrous power.

Nebuchadnezzar's civil religion presented a fresh crisis for Israel. For the Jews, participation meant blasphemy. Nonparticipation meant treason. How would the people of God respond to Babylon, this conqueror who had become a rather benevolent host? It would be downright rude to defy the King's command. More than that, it would be suicidal. And what good was a dead Israel? What use is a dead church?

Nevertheless, Shadrach, Meshach, and Abednego refused to worship Babylon's gods, no matter the cost. Had these three been ordinary Jews, they might have been safe. But since they held high positions of public office, their actions were viewed as treason against the state. Their resistance incensed the King, but the three resolutely kept their poise:

> O Nebuchadnezzar, we have no need to present a defense to you in this matter. If our God whom we serve is able to deliver us from the furnace of blazing fire and out of your hand, O king, let him deliver us. But if not, be it known to you, O king, that we will not serve your gods and we will not worship the golden statue that you have set up. (Daniel 3:16-18)

Their refusal to worship Nebuchadnezzar's statue was a bold act of open defiance against both Babylon's religion and its politics. This treason was punished by the state, but their courageous act of faith was rewarded by God, whom they refused to blaspheme. God delivered the three from the fiery furnace, and the great Nebuchadnezzar repented and gave praise to the God of Israel.

4. Robert P. Ericksen, *Theologians under Hitler* (New Haven and London: Yale University Press, 1985), p. 148.

Most people who have grown up in church families know the stories of the three men in the furnace and Daniel in the lions' den. My children are enthralled by them. But for most adults, the stories of these fearless four are dismissed as fables, no more relevant to life than Santa Claus. Even in many Christian families, the stories function primarily as entertainment. But their prophetic witness is no fable. And they are infinitely more than entertainment!

Spoken at a time of crisis for the Jewish people, they continue to speak. These stories are a word from the living God to a church under fire. They summon the church to reclaim its identity and destiny. They urge us to keep our bearings as we approach the twenty-first century.

The Bold Prophet of Patmos

Like the book of Daniel, the Revelation of John has often been misunderstood and misused. Commonly the happy hunting ground for end-time religious enthusiasts, it has been left by most Christians to those scholars and fanatics who appear to possess the key that unlocks its esoteric secrets. For most, Revelation remains tucked away at the end of the Bible, overshadowed by the more important letters and Gospels. Too few throughout the church's history have discovered that the book provides important direction regarding the church's life and mission during extraordinary times.

Revelation, like all biblical books, requires careful interpretation. But because of its special character, this book demands extraordinary care and responsibility. (The language and imagery were more easily understood by the original audience than they are by us.) Nevertheless, it *can* be understood. Even more, it *must* be understood. It carries an urgent message for the contemporary church,[5] a message with particular bearing on church families who wish to live faithfully and responsibly in today's world.

While I would prefer to avoid debate over the many ways to interpret the book, I must say at least this: biblically responsible interpretation positions the Revelation to John firmly in its first-century setting. Here is a pastoral letter written to Christians living in what is now modern Turkey, during the late first century. The author is a Christian pastor/prophet who penned a message from God while living in a federal prison camp on the island of Patmos. John was serving a sentence for political subversion; he stubbornly announced the rule of a King other than Caesar; he persistently proclaimed the rise of a Kingdom larger and more powerful than Rome. His message was not tolerated by the Empire.

Leaders were not the only ones confronted with this troubling religious-political situation. All those who bore the name "Christian" were part of the Roman Empire but could not be loyal subjects. Christians confessed Jesus, not Caesar, as Lord. Like the Jewish exiles in Babylon hundreds of years earlier, Christians found that their bold confession of faith led them into conflict with the state. But Jesus has not left them without guidance. John communicates a message from the Lord Jesus intended to strengthen and encourage a fearful and beleaguered church. At least this much can safely be said about John's message: the language and imagery and visions proclaim God's absolute victory and power, declare God's unmitigated judgment against the principalities and powers of sin and evil, and summon the church to faithfulness.

So similar was their situation to that of their Jewish ancestors who lived as exiles in Babylon that John freely named this new

---

5. M. Eugene Boring, *Revelation* (Louisville: John Knox Press, 1989), p. 1.

religious-political power with an ancient and memorable name: "Babylon."

> So he carried me away in the spirit into a wilderness, and I saw a woman sitting on a scarlet beast that was full of blasphemous names, and it had seven heads and ten horns. The woman was clothed in purple and scarlet, and adorned with gold and jewels and pearls, holding in her hand a golden cup full of abominations and the impurities of her fornication; and on her forehead was written a name, a mystery: "Babylon the great, mother of whores and of earth's abominations." And I saw that the woman was drunk with the blood of the saints and the blood of the witnesses to Jesus. (Revelation 17:3-6a)

John's thinking and praying were shaped by the Hebrew Scriptures. In the Old Testament, cities were often described as women. Jerusalem (also known as Zion) was described as a virgin (Isaiah 37:22), a daughter (Lamentations 2:13), a faithful wife and mother (Isaiah 66:7-14), a married woman who became unfaithful (Ezekiel 16). Nineveh and Tyre were both described as prostitutes (Nahum 3:1-7; Isaiah 23). The prophets used the image of a harlot to pronounce graphically God's judgment upon a city.

There is little doubt that the city John had in mind is Rome. The Romans worshipped many gods and goddesses. Like the Greeks before them who worshipped Athena as the Great Mother goddess, the Romans worshipped the goddess Roma. Archaeology documents the presence of temples to the goddess Roma in major cities throughout the Empire, including Ephesus, Smyrna, and Pergamum. (Christians living in these cities were specifically summoned to faithfulness earlier in John's Revelation.) For the Romans, Roma was venerated as the Great Mother goddess, giver of all blessings, the patroness of the city and the Empire. John's readers would have understood his startling allusion and its meaning immediately. In John's vision, the power of Rome is seen for what it really is. Stripped of all her glamor and sophistication, Rome is described not as a generous and nurturing mother, but as a seductive whore.[6] Talking about her in this way was anything but patriotic! Is it any wonder that their leader found himself shipped off to a Mediterranean Alcatraz? Is anyone surprised that Christians were often profoundly disliked? Occasionally featured in the Roman Colosseum as bait for Caesar's lions?

Identifying Rome (or any other political or religious power) as "Babylon," and describing that power as a prostitute, is a way of urging the church to resist seduction. Put another way, naming the powers serves to awaken the church from a false sense of security and from uncritically yielding to Rome or Washington, D.C. or Hollywood, and all they stand for — their values, politics, religion, worldview. John's vision assures judgment for those kingdoms that remain resolutely defiant before the Kingdom of God.

The painful memory of Rome's cruelty toward Christians under Emperor Nero in A.D. 64 was etched upon the minds of many. Some had experienced the bloodshed firsthand. The current persecution of John's churches at the close of the first century was mild in comparison. Few recognized it as merely the shadow of the high cost of discipleship for future generations. Emperor after emperor would make himself "drunk with the blood of the saints and the blood of the witnesses to Jesus" (17:6a) until Christianity became the state religion under Constantine in the fourth century. John's vision inspired the church to remain faithful to its message and mission, even in the face of imperial powers that persecute the people of God. The testimony of Christians in Nazi Germany or Communist China in our century proves the value of Revelation for situations resembling those faced by the church's earliest martyrs.

6. Ibid., p. 179.

To communicate this message of judgment and hope, the book of Revelation paints pictures. With the same purpose in mind, the book of Daniel tells stories. Revelation's author was a seer; Daniel's author was a storyteller. Revelation paints vivid pictures of God's victory and judgment; Daniel tells stories of courageous people who resisted the Empire. Both Revelation's pictures and Daniel's stories are intended for those with "ears to hear and eyes to see." These two books bear witness to a faith that becomes intensely relevant in the rugged reality of life and death. The Christian faith leads us into the market-place, and into conflict with powers, ideologies, myths, world-views, and assumptions that claim ultimate loyalty. The stories, prophecies, and visions of Daniel and Revelation challenge the church to remain vigilant, discerning the times in which we live, remembering the purpose of God fulfilled through his people — a people scattered among the foreign powers of the world. It is a call to bear witness to the reign of God even in the face of hostility and unbelief.

Naming the Powers

Daniel and Revelation are names of neglected, and too often misused, books of the Bible. Together, they carry an urgent message for the American church and the American Christian family. Christendom has collapsed; in its place rises a mighty city.

Babylon. Here is the city that illustrates the epitome of human arrogance; on this site humanity built a city and erected a tower that would reach to the heavens (Genesis 11:1-4).

Babylon. Here is the city that commemorates the confusion of the human condition; appalled by the peoples' arrogance, God made their speech unintelligible and scattered them far and wide (Genesis 11:5-9).

Babylon. Here is a name for a city that runs deep in the church's memory; it reminds us of the danger of apostasy and the need for faithfulness (Revelation 17:5).

Babylon. Here is that enlightened city which replaces biblical revelation with human reason and pagan revelry. In America today we are being systematically seduced into perceptions of reality and truth that are fundamentally foreign to the gospel. This is the Babylonian captivity of the contemporary church in North America.

The American Babylon is a capitalist society where deregulation allows virtually anyone and anything into the marketplace; why should it be different with religion? In faithfulness to the First Amendment, government has kept its hands off, and we are free to practice any religion we want. Almost. Through David Koresh and his Branch Davidians, Americans learned that there is a limit to bureaucratic tolerance and pluralism. There are some things even the American Babylon will not put up with.

That is the trouble. How does a pluralist society determine what is tolerable and what is not? This question stands at the core of today's debates over abortion, gay and lesbian rights, gender rights, racial/ethnic rights, public education, the environment, medical ethics, the American family. These issues identify the battle for America's soul, the struggle to define some common standard from which to structure society.

Consider the following example. In 1993 the AIDS Action Committee submitted a series of ads that were to be plastered on Boston's subways and trolleys. These condom ads were so explicit that the Massachusetts Bay Transportation Authority refused to run them. The Boston transit agency asked the AIDS Action Committee to redesign the ads. They thought posters with tag lines like, "One of these will make you 1-1,000th of an inch larger," and "Tell him you don't know how it will ever fit," contained "indecent sexual images." The AIDS Action

Committee disagreed, and sued. A district judge ruled that since the subways and trolleys are public forums, the MBTA must run the ads unaltered or violate the First Amendment.

Larry Kessler, executive director of the AIDS Action Committee, boasted that the ruling signaled the collapse of "yet another barrier erected by government officials more concerned about public relations than about public health."[7] Bold statement. Most agree that public health is more important than public relations. But do the ads really promote public health? It seems to me that public health means much more than helping people avoid AIDS.

I understand the judge's ruling on the case from a different angle. True, the ads may keep some from contracting a deadly disease; we may watch fewer of our friends, relatives, or neighbors die of AIDS. But I find a more deadly disease spreading among us. The ads, and our enforced tolerance of them, signal the spiritual and moral decay of American culture. Another sign of the times. I consider this decay a far deeper and more pervasive threat to public health.

My point is this: Kessler's boast reveals the bigotry of dogmatic pluralism. People are dying of AIDS. None of us wants people to die of AIDS. So we are told to say, "Wear a condom." But we must never say "Stop," or "Wait until you're married." And we must never, ever say, "Don't engage in homosexual practices." These are values, we're told. Mere values. And we must, above all, be tolerant. Values, opinions, and convictions are private matters. We are expected to keep them to ourselves. We may (for now, at least) espouse them in our families, churches, synagogues, or mosques. Our religious values are precisely that — *ours*. We are not to force them on those whose values may differ from ours. The public square is reserved only

7. William Raspberry, "The Flipside of Frankness," *The Washington Post* (Dec. 31, 1993), A21.

for the values commonly held by this modern liberal democracy — the values of celebrating and encouraging our diversity through tolerance and pluralism.

But I do not find much tolerance for my unwillingness to have children exposed to what I consider crude and offensive advertisements. My views are discredited because my appeal to moral decency comes from my religious convictions. My outcry is silenced because America chooses to protect politics from religious belief. We are told that the public world of politics deals with something called "facts," and the private world of religion deals with "values" and "opinions."

In his book *Culture of Disbelief: How American Law and Politics Trivialize Religious Devotion*, Yale law professor Stephen Carter reminds us that the idea of separating church and state was intended to protect "the church from the state — not the state from the church."[8] Our nation's Founders believed that the state should not be allowed to determine or interfere with the religious life of the people. This was one of the hard lessons learned in the struggle for religious freedom in Europe; it was the impulse for the holy experiment in the colonies. But none of the Founders believed that the state should or could insulate itself from the moral values of the people. They urged churches to be vigilant moral and political critics.[9]

What began as a détente has become a dogma. The separation of church and state was a handy truce, a type of mutual agreement that allowed religion and politics to co-exist without destroying each other. But in the process religion in America has been pushed to the periphery of public life. Tolerance and pluralism are names for those principles used to organize our

8. Stephen L. Carter, *The Culture of Disbelief: How American Law and Politics Trivialize Religious Devotion* (New York: Harper Collins, 1993), p. 115.
9. Ibid., p. 116.

modern belief system. And they are defended dogmatically. Under the power of this dogma the gospel is tamed and no longer can speak the truth that calls all rival conceptions of truth and reality to conversion.

The gospel may be personal, but it is never private. Our job is not simply to work as a benevolent chaplain to a society of competing individualisms; that is, we are not charged with winning people to a new view of private and domestic affairs — to *values* that are valid for some but not for others. Faithfulness to the message of the Kingdom of God, and his rule over all creation and all people, demands that we abandon the soggy marsh of privatized religion, and reclaim the higher ground of public truth.[10]

The simple act of naming our surroundings is among the first of our tasks. It helps us keep our bearings in this strange land. That's important. If we ignore the landscape in which we find ourselves, we lose our way. Failure to acquaint ourselves with our culture renders us faithless to our mission. But faithfulness requires more of us. We are not asked to live comfortably and safely in the land. We are sent on a mission that often requires us to live dangerously. A religious ghetto is fine for settlers content to live under the shadow of Babylon's soaring temples and awesome palaces. But God's pilgrim people will always press restlessly beyond despair or cynicism or self-centered complacency and into gospel-centered mission. The Bible has a name for this too. *Exodus*. It's a name we need to learn.

10. Lesslie Newbigin, *The Gospel in a Pluralist Society* (Grand Rapids: Eerdmans, 1989), p. 222.

CHAPTER 5

Exodus: Hope in God

JAMES is only four but his eyes have already seen too much. Emergency room examinations reveal multiple fractures in his arms and legs. Some are old, healed without proper medical care. He usually comes to preschool hungry, often poorly dressed during our long, cold winters. The boy's home is notorious among local social agencies. Trouble is, it's just one among many such households on our city's beleaguered West Hill.

James first came to our church through his foster parents. A month later the courts ordered him returned to his natural mother. The court also told his mother she must continue to take him to Kiddie Korner, our church's preschool. When he doesn't show, his teachers must contact the social worker immediately.

Accountability. Authorities hope it will help teach his mother responsibility. Our teachers hope it will keep James *alive*.

Recently, James came to school with a black eye. His brother apparently hit him with a baseball bat. "Just an accident," said James. The next week he sported another.

"What happened?" pressed his teacher.

"I don't remember," mumbled James.

Signs of abuse. Innocence stands shattered before our eyes.

58

We feel powerless, sometimes hopeless. These formative childhood years cannot be recaptured; we hope they can be redeemed. But we have James only a handful of hours each week; sometimes we wonder if our work makes any difference.

James carries a rather pungent odor with him wherever he goes. Hygiene isn't his mother's priority. Few children play with him . . . except Courtney. Courtney and James sit together on the floor building towers, or playing house in the Kid's Cottage. Courtney appears oblivious to the smell; she thinks he has pretty eyes.

And he does. Bright and blue, they seem to deny the dark and desperate saga unfolding behind the closed doors of his home. Behind those doors live an older brother, a younger sister, mom, and her live-in boyfriend. Here, drugs and alcohol are as common as Corn Flakes. The family is trapped, in more ways than one — enslaved to poverty, addiction, and a government handout. Welfare rewards James's mother for bearing children, remaining unmarried and unemployed.

"He's a bright child," says Carol, one of his teachers. "He's the one who could break out of the system. We don't think we can reach his mother. But we have hope for James. We can't *stop* hoping. He's too valuable."

James's teachers, standing in the presence of such need, battling against tremendous odds, remind us of the one thing the church must never stop doing. We must never stop hoping. Hope is the very bedrock of the news we're sent to spread. Hope in the present and coming Kingdom of God is the horizon toward which all of our efforts press.

Life at the Top

Since its beginning, America has generally been in an optimistic mood. Our nation was established on the fundamental promise that every American is guaranteed the right to "life, liberty, and the pursuit of happiness." No exceptions. The hope of the American Dream became a source of universal aspiration.

America blossomed in the decades following the Civil War. Transformed from an agricultural society to an industrial society, America became a land of unprecedented opportunity. Immigration surged. In 1854, nearly half a million immigrants stepped onto the shores of this promised land. In 1882, twice that many arrived. And by the early 1900s over a million Europeans streamed over our borders annually — more than the total number of immigrants to the thirteen colonies between 1607 and 1776.[1]

By 1890, the factory rather than the farm became America's chief producer of wealth. Millions poured into American cities. Chicago, New York, Boston, and Philadelphia exploded. Dirty and congested, the cities became jungles where millions worked to scratch out a living. The law of the jungle prevailed. For many, life was less than ideal. But determination, perseverance, and hard work often paid off.

Of course, not everybody was hopeful; but plenty were.

In Pittsburgh, for example, a thirteen-year-old Scottish immigrant found a job as a bobbin boy in a cotton factory. In 1848, he earned a dollar twenty a week. By the turn of the century, steel baron Andrew Carnegie owned and operated one of the greatest industrial enterprises in America. At retirement he was worth half a billion dollars.

Not far away, in Cleveland, a peddler's son worked as a clerk in a produce company. The year was 1855. John D. Rockefeller was just sixteen years old. Within twenty years, this enterprising young man had organized and built a business called the Standard Oil Company, and owned all the main oil refin-

1. Sydney Ahlstrom, A *Religious History of the American People* (New Haven and London: Yale University Press, 1972), p. 735.

eries in Cleveland, New York, Pittsburgh, and Philadelphia. He went on to become the world's richest man. By the time he died, Rockefeller had *given away* over half a billion dollars.

Stories like these inspired a nation. Millions read the stories of youngsters who started with nothing, faced all kinds of adversity, and ended up on top. Horatio Alger shaped a generation with books like *Strive and Succeed, Bound to Rise, Luck and Pluck, Brave and Bold.* He wrote over a hundred novels, and sold over twenty million copies.[2]

Rags to riches. It was the American Dream.

Like the nation, the church dreamed, too. Caught up in the optimistic mood, evangelical church leaders like Dwight L. Moody and John R. Mott stirred hundreds and thousands of young people to give their lives to the cause of world mission. Theirs was a dream worthy of sacrifice and commitment. "The Evangelization of the World in This Generation" was the slogan that tapped the hopes of America's youth, and triggered the greatest missionary enterprise in modern times.[3]

Liberal Christians, for their part, hoped to liberate Christianity from outdated, irrelevant, and downright pessimistic influences that stifled the human spirit. Sin was redefined as error, moral limitation, or oppression, which education or social reform could alleviate. Many modern Christians dismissed the traditional doctrines of original sin and human depravity as products of small minds and weak wills. Better to forget them. And the sooner, the better.[4]

At the turn of the century, most American Christians, conservatives and liberals alike, were intoxicated with the optimism of American culture.

2. Harry Emerson Fosdick, *The Living of These Days* (New York: Harper and Brothers, 1956), p. 46.

3. Ahlstrom, p. 864.

4. Ibid., p. 779.

But within a few short years, Archduke Ferdinand was shot and killed in Sarajevo, the capital of the Austrian province of Bosnia. World War I began. Its horror dealt a crushing blow to American optimism.

The Downward Spiral

The church did little to prepare Americans for the brutal events of the coming twentieth century. Instead, we unwittingly helped sow the seeds for widespread despair, cynicism, and complacency.

Standing at the close of this century, peering into the next, the Dream is fading. Today, yesteryear's slogans, "strike it rich," "there's always room at the top," "you can't keep a good man down," and "every man has a goose that lays a golden egg," are beamed into our living rooms in various forms and bantered about by media hucksters. But for a growing number of Americans, they ring hollow and distant, mere echoes of the past.

Today, we still hear echoes of the great evangelical slogans calling the church toward its mission, yet the world remains stubbornly resistant to the gospel. The Christian mission faces the proliferation of religion, the rising tide of militant Islam, and the spiritual apathy of secularism. Christianity is spreading, but not triumphant.

And that great temple of modern Christian theology? The liberal hope in the essential goodness of human nature and our innate ability to practice justice and live righteously lies in ruins — devastated by the horror of two World Wars, global starvation, rampant disease, economic chaos, and racial tribalization.

Still, our century hasn't been devoid of hope. On August 28, 1963, Martin Luther King, Jr. spoke passionately about hope from the steps of Washington's Lincoln Memorial. Before a quarter million people, the largest civil rights demonstration in history, King dreamed out loud for the nation.

> . . . I still have a dream. It is a dream deeply rooted in the American dream, that one day this nation will rise up and live out the true meaning of its creed — "We hold these truths to be self-evident, that all men are created equal."
>
> This is our hope. This is the faith that I go back to the South with. With this faith we will be able to hew out of the mountain of despair a stone of hope. With this faith we will be able to transform the jangling discords of our nation into a beautiful symphony of brotherhood. With this faith we will be able to work together, to pray together, to struggle together . . . knowing that we will be free one day.
>
> . . . And when we allow freedom to ring, when we let it ring from every village and hamlet, from every state and city, we will be able to speed up that day when all of God's children — black men and white men, Jews and Gentiles, Protestants and Catholics — will be able to join hands and to sing in the words of that old Negro spiritual, "Free at last! Free at last!
>
> Thank God Almighty, we are free at last!"[5]

King's preaching kindled hope. His vision pierced our prejudice. Digging deep into his own biblical tradition, King recalled the Exodus of God's people out of bondage and into freedom. He inspired Americans with the hope that things can change.

But the mood deep in America's urban ghettos was anything but optimistic. Just one year after King's speech, Harlem erupted in a four-day riot. And two years later, on the night of August 11, 1965, the Watts district of Los Angeles exploded. Rioting left thirty-five dead, 4,000 arrested, and an enormous

5. Quoted from Doris G. Kinney, *Life*, Special Issue: The Dream, Then and Now, "The Poetry of Protest: A Sampling of His Message, Which Rang Out Across the Nation" (Spring 1988), p. 9.

economic loss from arson and looting.[6] Unrest sparked similar riots in Chicago, Newark, and Detroit in succeeding years. Then almost thirty years later, when a black motorist was savagely beaten by five white police officers, Los Angeles again became a tinderbox for the unresolved racial tension still smoldering deep within our nation.

Today, King's dream seems to have gone flat. True, there's been plenty of progress. Blacks no longer surrender their seats to whites, or enter restaurants from the rear. African-Americans have gained substantial political power and made significant economic gains. But the grinding poverty in our cities remains largely black. And racism is anything but dead.

In fact, racial and ethnic tensions are escalating, not only in America, but around the world. In Bosnia, Serbian soldiers rape and murder Croatian women as part of their "ethnic cleansing" campaign. In the Middle East, a militant Jew storms a mosque and slaughters Muslim worshippers. In the Sudan, Muslim government troops withhold relief supplies from malnourished Christian children. In South Africa, white Christians threaten violence at the election of the nation's first black president. The Cold War is over, but we don't seem to be over war. Danger and crisis and chaos appear to run rampant. In Rwanda, over two million people fled their homes during the summer of 1994. 100,000 men, women, and children, mostly civilians, were killed within the first three weeks of civil war. David Syme, an American relief executive, says, "I've spent twenty years in Africa. I've seen it all. But I've never seen anything like this."[7]

Fortunately, America is a safer place to live. But some people wonder how much safer, and for how long. Many of our

---

6. Barbara Maddux, *Life*, Special Issue: The Dream, Then and Now (Spring 1988), p. 22.

7. "A Race with Death," *Newsweek* (August 1, 1994), p. 27.

homes have become centers for violence and abuse. Our streets have become war zones. Our schools have become arsenals. Some of our hospitals have become MASH units.

Racism, nationalism, economic chaos, and religious conflict are just a handful of the problems plaguing America and the world. Our world seems to grow more dangerous, chaotic, broken daily. We're more civilized, but our brains, our knowledge, and our progress have not brought an end to our ability to hate and hurt. Our technology has done immense good in the world around us but it has also handed us more sophisticated tools for brutalizing those we don't like.

The local community center is a great place for me to get my fingers on the pulse of my small part of America. When working out, I listen intently as the discussions touch on politics, the environment, education, religion, health, economics. What I hear isn't very encouraging. I hear frustration, fear, restlessness, sometimes anger. And it's not much different when I read *U.S. News and World Report*, or watch *NBC Nightly News*.

But I think the signs of growing hopelessness among our youth and young adults trouble me most. Pain punctuates their music. Consider these lyrics: "God is dead and no one cares/If there is a hell I will see you there." Grunge rock artist Trent Reznor howls these words at his listeners on his popular album, *The Downward Spiral*. Subsequent cuts slide from paranoia to murder, and finally suicide. The lyrics on the title cut include these lines: "He couldn't believe how easy it was/He put the gun into his face/Bang!/So much blood for such a tiny hole." This isn't music for the squeamish. There's nothing optimistic about it. It's grunge. Writes reviewer Guy Garcia, *"The Downward Spiral* is a 14-song, 65-minute howl of somebody falling into the void."[8]

The music characteristic of today's youth culture is not

8. Guy Garcia, "Nailism," *Time* (April 25, 1994), p. 81.

stuff from the fringe of American society. In the early 90s *Nirvana,* another grunge band, sold 10 million copies of its album *Nevermind,* knocking Michael Jackson's *Dangerous* from the top of the charts. Then its lead singer, Kurt Cobain, committed suicide. Like Horatio Alger a century ago, these artists speak for an entire generation. Maybe more.

Of course, not everyone is feeling such hopelessness, but plenty are.

For the most part, America's in a bad mood. Pessimism has replaced earlier optimism. Disillusionment is more common than hope. Apparently unable to bring change, many Americans are growing complacent, self-centered, apathetic. Others are becoming cynical. Some are downright desperate.

The twentieth century did not hand out the American Dream on a silver platter, nor did it usher in the Kingdom of God. Instead, it was filled with enough turbulence to sufficiently knock the air out of even the most resilient optimist.

The America Dream is exhausted, sucking air. Maybe America is finally ready to hear the gospel.

Hope in God

"What is the gospel?" I asked. It's a common word, one we throw around a lot in church. Acting on a hunch, I wanted to know how this class of young adults understood the word that stands at the very center of the church's life and mission. I was afraid that "gospel" was one of those words so overused it had lost it's meaning. I was right.

I got a number of interesting answers. And I learned a lot. Most of these men and women have attended church regularly from an early age. Most of them responded with nice, religious answers. But none of them told me what's *good* about this *news* we call the gospel. I was worried. If we can't describe the gospel,

I thought, we can't very well communicate it. Without the gospel the church becomes nothing more than a religious institution; church families become nothing more than paying members of a social club. With each answer I grew more discouraged.

Then a hand went up near the back of the classroom. "John, how would you describe the gospel?" I asked, desperate for something meaningful.

"Hope," he replied.

Bull's-eye. With just one word, John Apa gave us news worth spreading.

The Bible is full of hope, rich in gospel. The gospel culminates in Jesus Christ, but it doesn't begin there. In the beginning we learn that God created all things. What's more, we learn that God made all things "very good." People included. Genesis opens with an evangelistic sermon, a call to discipleship. In a world brimming with idolatry and crowded with religion, we're not left to wonder about God, our origins, our place and purpose in this world. Nor are we left to speculate. From the beginning we hear good news: God made us, God loves us, God provides us with meaningful work.

So much for good news. Bad news runs quick on its heels. Immediately after hearing the glad tidings of Creation, we come face to face with the Fall. The Serpent entices Eve, Eve entices Adam, the couple eats forbidden fruit. Disobedience shatters Eden's innocence, and life will never be the same. Nakedness becomes a shame, childbearing becomes a pain, and work becomes a chore. Families not only learn to fight, they learn to kill. These are the first fruits of sin.

Unfortunately, the bad news doesn't end there. Sin is contagious, and we're all infected. Look around. Sin remains earth's most devastating plague.

But if sin is contagious, so are other things: courage, laughter, enthusiasm, joy. Hope, too, is contagious. Since the beginning, God's people have never stopped hoping. We press restlessly forward, hoping in the righteousness, justice, and salvation of God. Though we are often forced to wait, God never disappoints us. God saves. Over and over again, the Bible spreads this news through the lives of some quite ordinary people.

And this salvation isn't just about what God did for one nation. Nor is it merely about what Jesus did for me, a sinner saved by grace. God's salvation is deeply personal, but it is never private; it's not the exclusive property of a single nation or race or denomination. The life, death, resurrection, and mission of Jesus Christ signals a new beginning for all creation, nothing less than the dawn of redemption, promised long ago, and whispered through the ages. In Jesus Christ, God liberates all things from bondage to sin and death (Romans 8:19-21), and reconciles all creation to himself (Colossians 1:20). This is the great victory shout of God!

In a world where apathy, cynicism, and despair are epidemic, we carry this gospel into the world, infecting others with the "germ of hope and liberation."[9]

But isn't this hope just wishful thinking? Aren't we just whistling in the dark?

Sometimes I wonder. The face of a battered four-year-old in our church's preschool stares into my own. Scenes of desperate Haitian refugees flash before my eyes: "If we die, we won't have to go to hell," says Jaures St. Hilaire in Port-au-Prince, "we're already there."[10] Hot tears sting my cheeks as I watch my mother's body lowered into the earth. Cancer is a cruel enemy; she was much too young to die. In times like these,

---

9. Jürgen Moltmann, *The Church in the Power of the Spirit* (New York: Harper and Row, 1977), p. 84.

10. Steve Komarow, "U.S. Urges U.N.: Back Haiti Action," *USA TODAY* (July 22, 1994), A1.

I need hope. In this rugged world, I need more than wishful thinking. I think others do too. We need to see signs of hope with our own eyes, feel hope with our own hands, hear hope with our own ears. Secondhand hope is little help.

There are a lot of things the church can do, but I think hope is the one best thing we can honestly offer the world. We're not just whistling in the dark. We have good reasons for hope. Consider these . . .

An aging shepherd finds himself standing barefooted before a burning bush, stunned by what he hears. "I've seen the misery of my people in Egypt," says God. "And I've heard their cry for help. I'm sending you to bring my people out of Egypt" (Exodus 3:7-10). God sends Moses to announce the Exodus and lead his people out of slavery and toward the Promised Land.

Exodus, Act One.

A lonely prophet wanders the rugged, windswept hills of the ancient Middle East. A voice breaks the silence. "Comfort, O comfort my people," says the Lord. "Speak tenderly to Jerusalem and cry to her that she has served her term" (Isaiah 40:1, 2a). God sends a messenger to prepare the Babylonian exiles for a new beginning — a new experience of God's grace after decades of exile and alienation. "In the wilderness prepare the way of the LORD, make straight in the desert a highway for our God" (Isaiah 40:3). "Depart, depart, go out from there! . . . For you shall not go out in haste, and you shall not go in flight; for the LORD will go before you, and the God of Israel will be your rear guard" (Isaiah 52:11-12). As the Lord once brought his people out of Egypt, he also rescued them from captivity in Babylon.

Exodus, Act Two.

A traveling preacher from Nazareth rides the dusty road into Jerusalem. Crowds along the parade route shout and dance. It's a scene packed full with meaning. Jesus' entry into the Holy

City on Palm Sunday consciously fulfilled an ancient hope. Zechariah prophesied this long ago: "Rejoice greatly, O daughter Zion! Shout aloud, O daughter Jerusalem! Lo, your king comes to you; triumphant and victorious is he, humble and riding on a donkey" (Zechariah 9:9). God rescued his people from slavery to Egypt. God delivered the exiles from Babylonian captivity. Israel hoped that once again God would hear the cries of his people — people living under the tyranny of Rome. They longed for another exodus. In Jesus, the New Testament declares, the God of Israel comes to save. Here is the King who comes in the name of the Lord to rescue his people.

Exodus, Act Three. God's final act.

Our hope is forged in the crucible of real life. God is no powerless idol crafted from stone or wood, decorating the tents of Middle Eastern nomads. Nor is God that mystical modern deity that stands aloof from the world watching from a distance. No. "The Word became flesh and lived among us, and we have seen his glory" (John 1:14). The God revealed to Israel and in Jesus Christ is rugged and real and active, not afraid to get dirty. God *acts*. God sees the plight of the poor, hears the cries of those who suffer, feels the pain of those who hurt.

I'm not sure I could believe in God if it were not for what I see and hear in Jesus Christ. In Jesus, God suffers with us in order to redeem us and bring a whole new world. God is not watching from a distance. It's the love of those who are willing to walk into my life and suffer with me that are most able to give me hope. So it is with God.

So I go on hoping that God is with us, often in ways we cannot understand. So I go on trusting that God has the power to bring good out of tragedy. God turned the horror of Good Friday's Cross into the wonder of Easter's Empty Tomb. The triumph of life over death, joy over sorrow, hope over despair, means that God is beginning to turn this old, dying world on its head. A whole new world is on its way. *That's* the Christian hope.

I'm not talking about escapism. Many think that's all Christianity offers . . . that we're so heavenly minded, we're no earthly good. That's tragic. The hope of this new creation empowers life in the midst of suffering. It makes for gutsy, courageous, red-blooded living. *Passion.* Like Jesus before us, we enter this world's suffering because we know suffering is not the last word.

Transforming Lifestyles

446 Santa Barbara Drive is the street address for a contemporary American mission outpost. From the outside, the house looks quite ordinary — just another upper-middle-class house in modern American suburbia. Inside, the home is anything but ordinary. For Grant and Rene Gereghty and their unique family, discipleship is a way of life; church is not something they attend, church is who they *are.*

Grant and Rene gave birth to three children: Sarah, David, and Daniel. When Daniel was eight, the family decided to open their home to foster children. The *family* decided — these decisions are democratic; everyone has a voice; all members share in this common mission. The family decided to *open their home* — their home is not a fortress, but a mission; all their children are committed to discipleship and the whole family enjoys sufficient resources to risk God's kind of loving: wild, extravagant, passionate, free. The family decided to open their home to *foster children* — this family believes that it's easier to build children than to repair adults. They draw their mission from Isaiah's words:

71

Is not this the kind of fasting I have chosen:
    to loose the chains of injustice and untie the cords of
        the yoke,
    to set the oppressed free and break every yoke?
Is it not to share your food with the hungry
    and to provide the poor wanderer with shelter —
    when you see the naked, to clothe him,
    and not to turn away from your own flesh and blood? . . .
Your people will rebuild the ancient ruins
    and will raise up the age-old foundations;
    you will be called Repairer of Broken Walls,
    Restorer of Streets with Dwellings.

                                        (Isaiah 58:6, 7, 12 [NIV])

Sonya and Steven, 15-month-old twins, were their first foster children. After an unsuccessful reunion with the birth family, the Gereghtys were asked if they would adopt the pair. They did. Since 1985, this family has helped restore hope and provide a fresh start for ten different children. Four of these kids had no other place to go. The family adopted them as their own.

Rene is convinced that hope and joy are contagious. So is courage and the willingness to risk. Her parents took in foster kids. Now she finds her family doing the same. Both Grant and Rene want their growing family to live on the edge, knowing God, trusting God, risking with God. They want to build children who are unafraid of the world around them . . . not naive, but brave. And it's working. From the beginning their children were intimately involved in this redemptive mission. Now they continue God's work. At 18, David traveled to Moscow. Today he's in South Africa.

In the beginning, the Gereghtys hoped to bring love and care and hope to a tiny pair of babies whose future was uncertain. God had something more in mind. That was the beginning of a great adventure. Along the way, they found themselves *transformed*.

72

Of course, the Gereghtys are unique, but they are not alone. They are one example of the work God, the Holy Spirit, is doing all around us. Transforming the lifestyles of ordinary people, God is launching a whole new mission to modern America. The center of this mission is not the building where the church gathers Sunday after Sunday. The mission centers in the homes and businesses and schools where church families live and work and learn each day.

These new American missionaries remember that we are exiles, strangers living in a land often hostile to the values and mission of the church. We practice exile by refusing to accept and assimilate into the changing world around us. But our stubborn resistance does not mean we retreat into a religious ghetto. Exodus lifts us beyond despair or cynicism or self-centered complacency and into an adventure marked by hope and joy.

The public nature of our mission will generally not take the form of disembodied pronouncements on the social, political, and moral issues of the day. Yes, we must challenge, in the name of the Lord Jesus Christ, the values, traditions, and truth claims of modern Babylon. But faithfulness requires more than words. Following God's lead, we will ruggedly engage ourselves in the lives of real people all around us.

The world doesn't need more busy people. Nor does it need more intelligent or gifted or effective people. The world doesn't even need more religious people. We desperately need more people like the Gereghtys. We need more *holy* people . . . men, women, and children courageous enough to enter into the apathy, cynicism, and despair — the *suffering* — of the world around us, and bring God's hope.

PART III

THE FAMILY ENGAGES GOD'S WORLD

CHAPTER 6

The Art of the Start:
Baptism, Marriage, and Singleness

THE NOISE shattered the stillness of the forest. Clang . . . clang
. . . clang. Birds tittered overhead. Squirrels scurried along the
branches of the maples and birches and pines. Chipmunks
wrestled on the forest floor. Evelyn worked alone.

Evelyn's son walked the path toward the noise. Dry leaves
crunched beneath his feet. Shafts of sunlight pierced the
shaded glen, and danced among the ferns and fallen leaves.

From a distance Bob watched his mother drive long metal
stakes into the soft earth. Those who knew Evelyn were accustomed to seeing her do what other women rarely do. In another
woman's hand, a hammer that size might have appeared
awkward. Not in Evelyn's. And it wasn't because she was large
or rugged. No. Evelyn embodied that rare combination of grace
and guts, more noble than elegant.

"You're wondering what your crazy mother's up to this
time," she said, wiping sweat from her brow. "Well, Bob, it's
time I start building my dream house."

Bob knew his mother too well to doubt her words.

Not long ago we buried Evelyn. Before her memorial service at the church, I gathered with her sons and daughters,

grandchildren, and great grandchildren in her home . . . her dream home, a testimony to Evelyn's Noah-like vision in the woods. Is this what her mind's eye saw that day when she marked off its foundation? As I stared out through the great panes of glass and into the woods she loved, I wondered if her retirement-ready friends thought her a bit daft at the time.

Her family had more stories, and I had mine. We laughed and we cried — all of us rather awed by the grandeur of this solitary human life. Often during those closing months of her battle with pancreatic cancer, I came to the house to serve communion, sing a few hymns, pray. But greater was her ministry to me. Sitting in her great four-poster-canopy bed, propped up with pillows, she said more than once, "I'm submitted and committed. Chris, what else do I need?" I couldn't think of a thing.

Evelyn died well. She died well because she knew how to live.

Holding the End in Full View

Evelyn was a visionary. Whether building her dream house or building a highly respected real estate business, raising children or battling cancer, from the start Evelyn held the end in full view.

We learn something valuable from a person like Evelyn. Evelyn lived her life *eschatologically*. So should every Christian. Eschatology is a technical term used by theologians to describe the Christian teaching about the future — not just tomorrow, but the End . . . capital *E*. The word *eschaton* is the Greek New Testament word for "the End," "the Last Thing," the consummation of God's purposes, the final chapter in the Christian Story.[1]

1. Dorothy and Gabriel Fackre, *Christian Basics: A Primer for Pilgrims* (Grand Rapids: Eerdmans, 1991), p. 167.

Whatever else Christianity teaches, it teaches that the future is not a closed book. Through Israel and in Jesus Christ, God gives us a glimpse of the future and invites us to live in the light of what we've seen. Our lives are characterized not only by faith and love, but by hope (1 Corinthians 13:13). And hope is what eschatology is all about. Talk of eschatology drives us back to what I've said before. We're pilgrims, not vagabonds. Vagabonds are tramps; they wander undirected by anything except a gnawing internal restlessness. Pilgrims are cut from a different cloth. Restlessness may characterize them, but a profound sense of purpose guides them. They are people on a mission. And from the start they know the direction they're headed.

We need people who know where they're headed. Trouble is, most families, including church families, haven't a clue. It's not so much that we can't see the future, we can't remember the past. And if we can't remember where we've come from, chances are we can't recall where we're going. Amnesia is debilitating.

I think God gives church families two key beginnings that not only cure amnesia, they help us glimpse the destination. Baptism is one, marriage is another. Both hold profound purpose for our lives. We forget them at our peril.

Baptism is the one thing all believers hold in common. Baptism and marriage are the two things all believing families hold in common. Baptism marks the start of our new life in Christ and in God's new Family, the church, while marriage marks the start of a new biological family — yours and mine. What happens in these two events — one sealed with water, the other with a kiss — sets the stage for what follows. In marriage, couples pledge themselves to one another. In baptism we are pledged to Christ. Both are exclusive: no other lover, no other Lord.

Neither a baptismal service nor a wedding ceremony is a

mere one-time event; they lay claim on us daily. The words, vows, prayers, and actions that fill these services help us remember where we've come from, and point us down the road. When each of us is baptized, we become Christians. When we live into that baptism, we grow toward full maturity in Jesus Christ. In short, we become *Christian*.[2] Likewise, when couples marry, they become married couples. But it's over the course of a lifetime that the "two become one" and they build a *marriage*. Both baptism and marriage are eschatological acts; they steer our families toward the End . . . capital *E*.

And knowing the End is the art of the start.

Heading for Trouble

Statistics tell us that over fifty percent of the marriages I witness this year will end in divorce. There's nothing good in that bit of news. I've sat with too many men and women whose lives are unraveling. Some of them are good friends. Divorce hurts. There's no way around it. And there's little to give me hope that we're getting any better at staying married.

When counseling engaged couples, I routinely ask about the couple's commitment to one another: "Do you plan to stay married?" They usually look at me as if I've asked if bees make honey. Yet they know what I'm after. The pain of divorce has touched both their lives in some way — parents, relatives, friends, co-workers. Someone they know is divorced. The question makes them nervous. Few of them have given it much thought. "Divorce won't happen to us," they assure me. "We *love* each other." They emphasize the word as if they have a

2. John Westerhoff, "Evangelism, Evangelization, and Catechesis: Defining Terms and Making the Case for Evangelization," *Interpretation: A Journal of Bible and Theology* (April 1994), p. 165.

special corner on the market. They don't. And I tell them so. Marriage is tough. Rewarding, but tough.

To make my point, I usually tell them my parable about river rock. "A stream polishes and rounds rough stones," I tell them, "but it takes years, years of tumbling and bouncing and buffeting by the current. In the end, all the rough, sharp edges are smoothed. No stone's left unturned, untouched, unchanged, no matter its size. Over the course of time, the river transforms the rock. So with marriage. I know of no better way for God to break our selfishness, pride, and independence than through marriage. Marriage polishes us. But it's never easy." Few of them seem impressed. But I hope some of them will remember when their lives begin to tumble.

I don't know anyone who begins married life expecting to fail. Many worry, but we all vow "till death do us part," or something like it. Still, half of us fail. Increasing numbers of Americans find themselves single again. A few couples meet in places like my pastor's study — angry, hurt, lonely, and frightened — before they meet in court. Most don't. Broken marriages, broken families, and broken lives litter the American landscape. It is not a pretty sight.

Sometimes the river shatters the rock.

Brokenness is a serious problem facing American families. Distrust is another. I don't know if distrust breeds brokenness, or if brokenness feeds distrust, but I'm certain they're related. Both point to our failure to live out our promises.

In 1985 a team of distinguished sociologists from the University of California published an important study about the loss of commitment among Americans. They called it *Habits of the Heart: Individualism and Commitment in American Life.* It was a landmark study a decade ago; its findings are perhaps even more accurate today. In their study, Robert Bellah and his team concluded that most Americans simply don't believe in commitment anymore. Instead, we believe in the individual's right to pursue personal fulfillment. We shy away from commitments that bind us to people or projects that don't promise us the happiness and satisfaction we feel we're owed.

I think they're right, but not entirely. Sure, I run into plenty of people who either avoid commitments completely or don't care enough to keep them. But every day I bump into others who believe in commitment, and hurt deeply when commitments fail. For them, the road of commitment-keeping is perilous, and sometimes they're tempted to call it quits. They don't want to, they just don't know if they can trust themselves and others to keep their promises. Commitment-keeping is risky business.

Brokenness and distrust do not foster an environment very friendly to marriage and family, or to community of any kind. They fray the invisible cord we call "commitment," a cord necessary for relationships not just to survive, but to thrive.[3] In this changing environment, the particular commitment we call "marriage" is no longer an option for a growing number of Americans. Homosexuals, single women, and even grandparents, among others, are challenging the definition and practice of the American family.

In July 1989, the New York State Court of Appeals granted official family status to a gay man who won the right to assume the lease of his deceased lover's Manhattan apartment. Similar state legislation and municipal ordinances have passed nationwide. More are on their way.[4]

Noel, a 37-year-old classical musician in Boston, is the mother of a 3-year-old daughter through artificial insemination. She speaks for a growing number of single women when she says, "Most of us wanted to be married and have children in a

3. Cf. Lewis Smedes, *Caring and Commitment: Learning to Live the Love We Promise* (New York: Harper and Row, 1988), p. 1.

4. Jean Seligmann, "Variations on a Theme," *Newsweek*, Special Issue (Winter/Spring 1990), p. 38.

more traditional way, but it just didn't work out. Then we hit those age deadlines and we can either make the choice of having children on our own or never have the experience of having a family." Caught between a rock and a hard place, Noel picked a sperm donor, and started her family.[5]

And there are other forms of nontraditional families. When parents either can't or shouldn't take care of their kids, grandparents find themselves in the parenting role . . . again. Ruth Rench is one of them. In her retirement, Ruth planned to travel using the savings she'd built after twenty-five years with the local school system. When her three-year-old granddaughter hinted that she'd been molested by one of her mom's male friends, Ruth put those plans on hold, permanently. After two years and $25,000 she won custody of her granddaughter. She's not alone. Rench and her granddaughter are part of a new phenomenon of "skip generation" families, members of the Fort Worth, Texas, area chapter of Grandparents Raising Grandchildren.[6]

These are just a few of the ways the family is changing. Christendom no longer shapes our vision of marriage and family life, and the whole concept of family is consequently being redefined. Many of our contemporaries, happy to throw off the yoke of Judeo-Christian tradition, hope to forge a brand new purpose and practice for family and community life in a post-Christian America.

For one thing, the modern family does not necessarily begin with marriage. In fact, marriage may no longer serve any real purpose in these newer definitions of family and community life.

Christians who are serious about the gospel won't condemn these changes as immoral, berate them as irresponsible,

5. Ibid., p. 44.
6. Ibid., p. 46.

or dismiss them as irreligious. Most Americans are doing the best they can with the information they have. Their efforts to shape values and build communities are consistent with a particular worldview. That it happens to be at odds with the one handed to us in the gospel isn't their fault. The gospel is *news*, not common sense (Romans 10:14-17). God's coming new world, announced in the gospel, is entered only through conversion. If there are fools in America, it's not those who reject our way of living. The real fools may be those of us who are seduced into believing that anyone should or could enter God's new Kingdom without the new birth.

Yes, we are, as a culture, headed for trouble. Alas, the real trouble is not so much with America, but with the church. I'm afraid that for too long we've allowed the surrounding culture to prop up our lifestyles. We can do so no longer; perhaps we never should have done so in the first place.

When it comes to marriage, family, and community life, Americans are eager for direction. Social prophets peddle their wares in the arts and music, on the written page and on the stage. The church must speak too. Engaging this fresh opportunity for evangelical witness, the church practices and proclaims the gospel's peculiar style of marriage and singleness birthed in the waters of baptism and nurtured by Scripture.

The Genesis of the Family

So, where do we start? We start with these words: "In the beginning God . . ." (Genesis 1:1). The Bible starts here for a reason. From the beginning, the Bible writes the word "God" in large letters. God eclipses all creation and all history. Creation derives its identity and destiny from *God*, nothing else. From the start God calls the shots, not we; God's purpose matters more than our own; God's work takes precedent over ours.

Such talk propels us toward a collision. We live within a culture that begins and ends with ME. If we make room for God at all, we'll have God on *our* terms, thank you. The opening words of Genesis confront our arrogance. God will be had on no other terms than God's. A confrontation is unavoidable. Furthermore, it is intentional. By his Word and Spirit, God intends to give shape to a peculiar people whose lives witness to God's design for all life. God sends his witnesses into cultures brimming with idolatry — nations, communities, and families whose lives are shaped by varying stories of the origin and purpose of the cosmos and its history: Hindu, Buddhist, Native American, African animism, and modern western secularism, to name just a few. These stories often vary significantly from the Story begun here in Genesis. Conflict is inevitable.

Near the beginning, the Story tells us that "God created humankind in his image, in the image of God he created them; male and female he created them" (Genesis 1:27). Scholars debate a good deal about the meaning of this verse, but we can safely say at least this: by nature, God made us social beings. "We are so unshakably created for community," says social scientist Mary Stewart Van Leeuwen, "that we cannot even develop as full persons unless we grow up in nurturing contact with others."[7]

Furthermore, God created us for meaningful interaction with the opposite sex. Marriage is not accidental. The relationship shared between a man and a woman is no mere social convention; it's part of the fabric of creation itself. The unity shared between husband and wife reveals the image of God. Does this mean that people must marry in order to experience fulfillment? Does it mean that singles cannot bear God's image? No. But it does mean that in singleness we can miss that

---

7. Mary Stewart Van Leeuwen, *Gender and Grace: Love, Work, and Parenting in a Changing World* (Downers Grove: InterVarsity Press, 1990), p. 41.

particular form of intimacy experienced between men and women. In a culture so confused about this key relationship, and often broken because of it, this is especially evident.

Marriage is an eschatological sign. It characterizes the harmony of Eden's paradise. That first pair lived together, working, playing, and loving side-by-side in perfect friendship with one another, with creation, and with God. The Story tells us that they were "naked and unashamed." No walls, no brokenness, no violence. Adam and Eve led all creation in obedience to God.

This is the End toward which marriage presses us. Marriage is a sign of hope, anticipating that Day when we stand "naked and unashamed" again before God, creation, and one another . . . that Day when we enjoy perfect union between Jesus Christ and his church . . . that Day when God will set all things right again. Sin, death, and evil conquered forever, God will dismantle our walls, heal our brokenness, silence our violence.

Have any of those starry-eyed engaged couples hinted at all this when I ask them why they want to marry one another? No. And it's no real surprise. Few of us think about marriage and family along these lines. We don't naturally grasp this kind of vision for marriage and its purpose in family life, nor do we grapple with the Bible's broader vision for marriage and family life within the experience of God's new Family, the church.

The Genesis of God's New Family

When we come to the New Testament, we learn that marriage and family don't really play a significant role. In fact, the New Testament doesn't seem to share our rather strong feelings about them at all. This discovery is unsettling, but true. Most often when Jesus speaks about marriage and family, he does so to show how authentic discipleship can actually *endanger* these cherished relationships.

From the very start, discipleship is dangerous to our marriages and families. The opening chapter of Mark's Gospel illustrates this. Jesus, baptized, then tempted by Satan in the wilderness, and now preaching the gospel, walks along the Sea of Galilee. He sees a pair of fishermen, Simon and his brother Andrew. "Follow me, and I will make you fish for people," he shouts. Sounds a bit crazy. The crazy thing is not what Jesus says, but what these two fisherman do. They drop their nets, leave their boat and family business, and follow Jesus.

Maybe there was more to it than this. Maybe they didn't leave everything all at once. Maybe they continued to fish, providing enough income to provide food and clothing for their wives and kids. Maybe they didn't. Mark is not concerned to tell us these things. He is concerned to show us the drastic immediacy of their response: "And immediately they left their nets and followed him" (Mark 1:18).

Then, not more than a quarter-of-a-mile down the beach, Jesus spies two more fishermen. Instant replay. James and John drop everything and get into line behind Simon and Andrew. Their father Zebedee is left holding the nets, staring dumbfounded at this rag-tag group of dreamers. Just like that, his two sons walk out on him *and* the family business. I doubt they left with his blessing.

Is discipleship really as helpful to our marriages and families as we Americans wish? I think the Gospel according to America makes both Jesus and discipleship all too tame. Our Americanized gospel involves very little risk. Membership in our churches costs us nothing, demands next to nothing. We come and go as we please, more like patrons of a social club than partners in our Lord's missionary enterprise. True, the gospel is free, but it's never without cost. It may well cost us our safety, our security, our sloppy self-confidence.

On another occasion, Jesus is home. But not with his family. He's living with friends, perhaps in the home of Simon and Andrew in Capernaum. As he teaches, there's a knock at the door. His mom is there, and she's not alone. With her are Jesus' brothers. They're concerned about him; they think he's lost his marbles. He's gone "out of his mind," the story tells us (Mark 3:21). They've come to take him home, back to reality, back to the safety of his family.

One of Jesus' new friends opens the door. "Jesus, your family is here. They want a word with you."

"Who is my family . . . my mother and my brothers?" Jesus asks. Then looking at those who sat around him, he says, "Here are my mother and my brothers! Whoever does the will of God is my brother and sister and mother" (Mark 3:31-35). Jesus *is* home, thank you.

Later in his ministry, Jesus will stress all this once again: "Whoever comes to me and does not hate father and mother, wife and children, brothers and sisters, yes, and even life itself, cannot be my disciple. . . . none of you can become my disciple if you do not give up all your possessions" (Luke 14:26, 33).

Great, just what we need: more broken families. And just when we started looking to Jesus to help us keep our troubled families together!

I know a seminary professor who regularly opens one of his classes by reading a letter from a father to a government official. The father complains that his son, who received the best education, went to all the right schools, and landed a good job as a lawyer, got mixed up with a weird religious sect. This sect controlled his every move, told him whom to date and whom not to date, and took all his money. The father pleads with the government official to do something to stop this dangerous religious group.

Who's this letter describing? The Moonies, David Koresh and his Branch Davidians, some other cultic group? No. It's a composite letter drawn from the actual letters of third-century Roman parents concerning a group called the Christian church.[8]

Though in many ways the New Testament deeply values marriage and family, it doesn't focus on them. It focuses on *baptism.*

Baptism, Marriage, and Singleness

When I was baptized, my parents took me to a church in downtown Boulder, Colorado. My parents were doing what most parents in the 1950s and '60s were doing — taking their newborns to local churches for a ritual part of American religion. My grandfather, a Methodist pastor from Florida, was granted the privilege of dousing me with water, laying his hands upon my head, and praying. Few of us really knew what was happening. In baptism, I was adopted into a new family, a very large one. I didn't choose my new brothers and sisters, mothers and fathers. I didn't even choose God. All this was chosen *for* me.

Baptism is a picture of the gospel. We are saved by grace alone. The gospel is about what God has done for us, not what we do for God. Baptizing babies paints this truth in vivid color. Babies can't hold a job, earn a paycheck, or contribute meaningfully to society. They are a liability (I think that's exactly why we love them). The gospel declares that whether we're black or white, old or young, wise or foolish, healthy or sick, this is how we come to God: as utterly dependent children. Baptism, whether received early in life or farther down the road, shows us how all of us enter God's new Family — through a second birth.

8. William H. Willimon, *Peculiar Speech: Preaching to the Baptized* (Grand Rapids: Eerdmans, 1992), p. 119.

In one sense, baptism did nothing to save me. Water splashed on the head of a sputtering infant isn't some sort of pagan magic, even if the act is attended by a good dose of holy prayer. As a baby, I was still not a Christian. But in another sense baptism did everything to save me. For in that act, I was handed gifts: the gift of adoption (I could live my life as a member of Jesus' family), and the gift of vocation (I could give my life in service to Jesus Christ). As I grew, the church helped me unwrap these gifts and receive them as my own. God's gifts saved me. They save us all. They save us from loneliness and boredom, and set us on the high road of gospel adventure.

Baptism opens the door for a broader understanding and practice of family life — one truly revolutionary, not only in the ancient world, but also in our more modern one. Family life lived from the perspective of God's Kingdom signals the new beginning promised in the gospel, and demonstrated in baptism.

We begin to see the power of baptism when we realize how it transforms the lives of those who have no real family. . . .

Not long after the Resurrection, the Holy Spirit pressed the early church into the Judean countryside. An angel sent Philip on a mission. He had no idea what he would find along the way. He had no idea of the strange ways God intends to grow his Family, the church. Philip only knew he must go. On the way, God engineered a chat between Philip and an Ethiopian traveler. Maybe you remember the story.

The Ethiopian is no ordinary traveler. The man has been to the Jewish city Jerusalem to worship the Jewish God. He reads the Jewish Bible. But he's a eunuch. And that poses a problem, a big problem. "Eunuch" means he's lost something, something essentially *male*. Not only has he lost a part of his body, he wonders if he's lost part of his soul.

The Hebrew Bible he is reading is quite clear, "No one whose testicles are crushed or whose penis is cut off shall be admitted to the assembly of the LORD" (Deuteronomy 23:1). Sexless by accident, or choice, or royal decree, this eunuch will never have a family of his own, and there is no place for him in God's Family. "Throughout Scripture children are praised as a reward from God, a sign of divine blessing," author William Willimon reminds us. "But this eunuch will never have children, will never have a family and therefore will have no place in the family of God. He can never enter the temple and praise God with the rest of us who have been blessed by God with family."9 He has no family. He has no church.

But that's not the end of the story. Philip is God's messenger who announces news to this eunuch . . . *good news.* "Let me tell you about Jesus," says Philip. "Like you, he had no family, no children. He, too, was excluded, tossed out of the Temple. They even killed him. But they didn't stop him. God raised him up, and through him is creating a whole new family . . . *the largest family this world's ever seen.*" (Willimon helped me understand the story this way.)

"And no one can keep me from joining up?" asks the eunuch.

"No one."

"God wants to adopt *me?*"

"*You.*"

There, in the desert, Philip found enough water to baptize him in the name of the Lord Jesus Christ. White and black, Jew and Ethiopian became family . . . on the spot.

I'm afraid that most American Christians hold a vision of family that is simply too small. "Family" too often refers to those families that begin with marriage rather than baptism. Couples will not, and should not, stop marrying. Marriage has great significance for Christians. But neither should Christians avoid singleness or view singleness as a mere transition to

9. Ibid., p. 121.

marriage and parenting. And we certainly must not view single-ness as an unfortunate final stage endured by white-haired widows or balding widowers.

Baptism, not marriage and the traditional family, is the universal condition of all Christians. According to the *gospel*, family begins with baptism. In the church, widows and orphans, infants and geriatrics, single parents and adults who never married, mingle with couples and children of all ages. "Here are your brothers and sisters, parents and children," says Jesus. Here is a whole new family birthed in the waters of baptism, a family that knows that we are related by hope, not biology, a family that remembers that our true home is not the biological family, but the church.[10]

For some, that's frightening. So be it. But for people like Jill and Martin, it's good news.

When Jill and Martin married they dreamed of raising a family. She often pictured herself pregnant, changing diapers, getting kids off to school. Martin dreamed of coming home to kids in the yard, dropping his brief case and tossing the ball with a son. Ten years later, they still weren't pregnant. They'd tried everything, even adoption. The waiting list seemed end-less. They were crushed. Infertility ended their dreams for family.

In the summer of 1990, Jill and Martin signed on with a crew from their church for a short-term mission to Mexico. Traveling was nothing new for the couple. On their honeymoon, they'd seen Europe, but in Mexico, they *lived among the people*. Big difference.

Diane Davis and her organization "Constructores para Christo" build homes. But that's not all. They link short-term missionaries like Jill and Martin with the families who will live

---

10. Stanley Hauerwas, *After Christendom?* (Nashville: Abingdon Press, 1991), p. 128.

in these homes. They work together, eat together, worship together. They build much more than a shelter for one family. The house itself is part of a growing gospel-mission to the greater community. The family belongs to a local church, and their new home becomes a mission outpost.

They also build a relationship. And it's life-changing. Working alongside one such family, Jill and Martin saw more than the family's economic poverty, they glimpsed a kind of treasure money cannot buy. They were confronted with a larger vision for the family of God. The couple was thunderstruck. "Through our new Mexican friends my eyes were opened," says Jill. "There's more to God's world than the place we're living. There's more to family than just the two of us. God's people are everywhere. We *must* be with them . . . *we're family now.*"

In the fall of 1994, this childless couple arrived in Africa, set up home, and began a new life in Mozambique. They are teaching in the church, and ministering among the tens of thousands of parentless refugee children.

Baptism. In God's new Family, this childless couple has many children, and many parentless children have parents. Together they're members of *the largest family this world's ever seen.*

Meanwhile, Americans tinker around with marriage and family life. We attend workshops, read books, pay therapists. There's nothing necessarily wrong with this kind of tinkering. It may do some good. But I'm afraid that our tinkering reveals a deep lack of vision, a poverty of purpose. We are too often bored rather than bold. Unless we all, old and young, married and single, are gripped by an adventure so compelling that we lose our sense of self-interest and self-preservation, our families will remain disintegrating rather than integrating forces for Christ's Kingdom in this world.

In baptism we glimpse the destination, and embark on an adventure. After they have been washed and raised to new life

93

in Christ, God not only adopts "saints from every tribe and language and people and nation" into his new Family, he sends them in mission: "a kingdom and priests serving our God, and they shall reign on earth" (Revelation 5:9, 10).

Knowing the End is the art of the start.

CHAPTER 7

Life Together: On Becoming Real

As I write, our boys, Joshua and Jeremy, are still young enough to allow Julie and me to organize our lives together around a fairly predictable routine. Evenings, for example, are simple: dinner, playtime, baths, pajamas, teeth, story time, prayer, lights out . . . and yes, one *last* drink of water!

Storytime's a favorite. Bible stories, Disney stories, classics like *Goodnight Moon* and *Winnie the Pooh.* These are precious moments. The boys often listen with rapt attention, snuggled in their blankets, cradling a stuffed bunny or Barney.

Though the routine is simple, it's not necessarily easy. Especially on those nights when a meeting for me means Julie handles things alone. And then there are occasional evenings when tempers fray, stories go unread, children pout in their beds, and if I'm not at a meeting, I wish I were.

It was on one of *those* nights that Margery Williams's marvelous story *The Velveteen Rabbit* went to work on me. As the whining and whimpering faded away into silence, Julie and I picked up the house. I was complaining about how tough parenting can be. There in a corner lay the book. I sat down, book in hand. The storybook stared up at me, so perfect, so innocent, so . . . unreal. A book can't talk back, bite, throw things. It can't disobey. If I don't like it, I can shut it and shelve it. The reader's always in charge.

"That's not *real* life," I thought.

I shut the book. There on the cover was a different sort of picture. A tattered bunny, whiskers crumpled, one ear flopped. He looked the way I felt. I fanned the pages of the book. I remembered my childhood days listening to my mother read the story. I remembered my stuffed bunny. He went with me everywhere, for what seemed ages, until that fateful day when his seams burst and his stuffing fell out. Bunny was finally beyond repair.

My eyes stopped at the top of page ten, arrested by these words: " 'What is REAL?' asked the Rabbit one day." Funny, I didn't remember the bunny asking such adult questions. As I reread the conversation between the Velveteen Rabbit and the old Skin Horse, I began to wonder if Margery Williams wrote more for whining parents than for their sleeping children . . .

> "Real isn't how you are made," said the Skin Horse. "It's a thing that happens to you. When a child loves you for a long, long time, not just to play with, but REALLY loves you, then you become Real."
>
> "Does it hurt?" asked the Rabbit.
>
> "Sometimes," said the Skin Horse, for he was always truthful. "When you are Real you don't mind being hurt."
>
> "Does it happen all at once, like being wound up," he asked, "or bit by bit?"
>
> "It doesn't happen all at once," said the Skin Horse. "You become. It takes a long time. That's why it doesn't often happen to people who break easily, or have sharp edges, or who have to be carefully kept. Generally, by the time you are Real, most of your hair has been loved off, and your eyes drop out and you get loose in the joints and very shabby. But these things don't

matter at all, because once you are Real you can't be ugly, except to people who don't understand."[1]

Slowly, I began to understand. I realized the wisdom of the old Skin Horse. I realized that our world is full of phony people on their way from here to who knows where; phony people who "break easily, or have sharp edges, or who have to be carefully kept." And too often, I'm one of them. Like the Rabbit, I longed to be Real, for my family to be Real. Yet I didn't relish the idea of growing shabby and losing my eyes and getting loose in the joints. I wished we could become Real without the mess, and without the pain.

The Families God Chooses to Use

Most families suffer no illusions — life together is rarely tidy, simple, predictable. Trouble is, we're uncomfortable with that . . . deeply uncomfortable. Come right down to it, we want storybook families: perfect and innocent, no real surprises in the plot. We want kids and spouses and relatives who don't talk back, bite, throw things. We want harmony. Maybe we wish we had more control. Sorry, *The Velveteen Rabbit* warns, there are no shortcuts to becoming Real.

Too often we pick up the Bible the same way I picked up my boys' storybook. The Book stares up at us, so perfect, so holy, so . . . unreal. Black leather, pages trimmed with gold, acid-free paper. After a fight with a spouse or kids, an argument with mom and dad, we hardly feel worthy to read the words. Too bad, for if we stick with it long enough we learn that Real isn't something that happens all at once. We become real as

1. Margery Williams, *The Velveteen Rabbit* (Kansas City: Ariel Books, 1991), p. 10.

we live this life together . . . with each other . . . with God. It takes a long time. And it doesn't usually happen to families who break easily, have sharp edges, have to be carefully kept, or need things tidy, simple, predictable.

We learn that this Story, like the story of *The Velveteen Rabbit,* is a Story of redemption. It's a Story of becoming. It's the Story of a family that not only grows to become the largest family this world has ever seen — God's Kingdom Family — but all along the way this Family must learn and relearn to become Real people who follow a Real God. That's never easy, and it's rarely tidy.

Take Abraham, for example. His name means "father of a multitude," and he's the head of a family, a very large one. Jews and Muslims trace their heritage to this one man. So do Christians. The Apostle Paul argues that everyone who believes the gospel is a descendant of Abraham (Galatians 3:7). We might assume that the father of these great world religions was the epitome of faithfulness, one truly worthy to be used by God. We might assume the same of his family. Real saints, every one. Well, the Bible shatters our assumptions; its saints aren't necessarily ours.

Behold Abraham. He heard God say, "Go from your country and your kindred and your father's house to the land that I will show you" (Genesis 12:1). So he went. Just like that, he struck out in obedience toward the Promised Land — much to the dismay of his family, against the good advice of his friends. Abraham followed this odd God whom no one had seen, and whom no one but Abraham had heard.

"Abraham, you sure it wasn't just the howling of the wind?"

"I'm sure."

"Maybe a heifer in labor . . ."

"No. The Voice said, 'I will bless those who bless you, and the one who curses you I will curse; and in you all the families of the earth shall be blessed.' Wind doesn't talk. Cows don't bless."

Courageous Abraham. Israel remembers him as a righteous man, a real saint. So does the church. Abraham: here's the saint who lied to Pharaoh to save his skin; "Sarah's my sister, not my wife," he said . . . *Cowardice.* Abraham: here's the saint who slept with his wife's maid, Hagar, and produced his first son, Ishmael . . . *Impatience.* Abraham: here's the saint who climbed Moriah's lofty crags, prepared to sacrifice his son Isaac in reckless obedience to God's command . . . *Faith.*

Faithful Abraham had his flaws. So did his family.

His grandson Jacob stole something money can't buy; he stole his older brother's birthright. Later, Jacob pilfered Uncle Laban's flocks and household, helped himself to Laban's choicest daughter Rachel, then ran off with Laban's daughters, grandchildren, cattle, even his household gods. He's a man marked by cunning and deceit.

What goes around, comes around. Jacob's family gave him problems of his own, the kind of problems his harried father probably wished on him: "Jacob, someday I hope God gives you a son who causes you as much grief as you've caused me." Jacob's twelve sons tossed his beloved son Joseph into a pit, then sold him to Midian merchants on their way to Egypt. Jacob's heart broke.

Is God Foolish?

Here's a family not much different from most of the families I know. Of course, it's true that spiritual apathy characterizes a good number of those families attached to the church. But plenty of others deeply desire to live faithfully. It just that life sometimes makes faithfulness intensely difficult.

My friends, Bob and Alma Foltz, know this firsthand. Years

ago, they lost their son, a budding young man, in a senseless motorcycle accident. As life has worn on, their children's families have faced their share of pain and problems too. Most recently, Bob has battled cancer. "Sometimes you gotta tie a knot in the end of the rope and hold on," they tell me.

For families like the Foltzes, the stories from Genesis are gospel material. No matter how much pain and how many problems intrude, no matter how we may bumble our God-given mission, God will have his way. Through Abraham and his family, "all the families of the earth shall be blessed" (Genesis 12:3). The Promise still stands.

We learn from these stories what I've learned through experience: God best uses those people and families least conscious of being used, those least aware of their worth. Sometimes God uses those least eager to be used. The Bible doesn't hold up some got-it-all-together family as the paradigm of faithfulness and usefulness. Quite the contrary. The Bible demonstrates the embarrassing fact that this odd God uses the oddest people: Abraham, Jacob, Peter, you . . . me.

Is God a *fool*?

Doesn't God know what kind of people fill our families, what kind of families fill our churches, what kind of churches dot this planet?

Is God *blind*?

Can't God see what's going on inside our families and churches? Can't God see what Christians are doing to tarnish his name, jeopardize his mission to the world?

Apparently the Apostle Paul wrestled with the same questions, especially in his relationship with the troubled believers and their families who gathered Sunday after Sunday as the church at Corinth. Paul had hard words for this beleaguered group. Much of his letters is made up of instructions for their life together. "Shape up!" he commands throughout these letters. "Get your lives together! Practice a lifestyle congruent with the gospel!" But he never once implied that their troubled lives placed God's redemptive mission in jeopardy. In fact, the problems created by life together in the church family became the lens through which the world would see the gospel message (2 Corinthians 4:7). Maybe life together was chaos, but they were on their way to becoming *real* messengers of the gospel.

God is no fool. God needs no glasses.

Here's what Paul told them: "The Message that points to Christ on the Cross seems like sheer silliness to those hell-bent on destruction. But for those on the way of salvation it makes perfect sense. This is the way God works, and most powerfully as it turns out" (1 Corinthians 1:18).[2]

To make his point, Paul quoted from the prophet Isaiah, a text that warns against taking human wisdom too seriously. "It's written," continued Paul, "'I'll turn conventional wisdom on its head, I'll expose so-called experts as crackpots'" (Isaiah 29:14).

Then Paul pressed the point home. "Human wisdom is so tiny, so impotent, next to the seeming absurdity of God. Human strength can't begin to compete with God's 'weakness.' Take a good look, friends, at who you were when you got called into this life. I don't see many of the 'brightest and the best' among you, not many influential, not many from high-society families. Isn't it obvious that God deliberately chose men and women that the culture overlooks and exploits and abuses, chose these 'nobodies' to expose the hollow pretensions of the 'somebodies'?" (1 Corinthians 1:25-28).

What makes perfect sense to God, makes little sense to us.

2. I'm drawing here from Eugene Peterson's fresh translation of the New Testament, *The Message: The New Testament in Contemporary English* (Colorado Springs: NavPress, 1993), p. 339.

Exposing Fraud

Some people can't stomach all this. Some people want a God who's tidy, simple, predictable. They want church and family life the same way. The message of the gospel — this odd God who saves and uses odd people in such an odd way — gives them indigestion. That's nothing new. From the dawn of time, people have cooked up gods more palatable to their weak stomachs. And it's not just people outside the church who do this. We Christians have done it too.

Almost from the beginning, some Christians found the sufferings and humanity of Christ distasteful. They figured that if Christ truly suffered he could not be divine. They concluded that if Christ were truly divine he could not possibly suffer. They worked out an elaborate theological system that assured believers that Christ remained untouched by the struggle and pain of being truly human and living on this broken planet. Christ is pure God, undefiled by human flesh and blood, a savior who lifts us out of this muck we call everyday life.[3] In other words, Christ was truly God, but not truly human.

Both our Apostles' and Nicene Creeds opposed this heretical teaching, which they named "Docetism." The Definition of Chalcedon in A.D. 451 made explicit the Christian teaching that Jesus Christ is both "truly God" *and* "truly human."

So what? What's this have to do with my family and me? Glad you asked.

I'm afraid a dangerous docetic heresy lurks among American church families today, not just in our views of Jesus Christ, but in the way we live our lives together as his disciples.

---

3. St. Ignatius (early 2nd century A.D.) combats this heresy in his letter *To the Trallians* 9.10, quoted in *Documents of the Christian Church*, ed. Henry Bettenson, 2nd edn. (New York and London: Oxford University Press, 1963), p. 35.

Our families and churches are not just places to belong, they're places to become. They are places where we grow into our baptism, becoming fully devoted followers of Jesus Christ. Here we can pull off our masks, remove our makeup, strip off our put-on smiles. These are places where we can be real with one another. Unfortunately, these places are too often the very places we most *avoid* when we're busted and flat on our backs. These are the very people among whom we feel we must wear masks and makeup, and by all means wear a smile. Here, we must appear to have-it-all-together.

Docetism.

We've believed a lie. The Devil has seduced us into believing that God can't really mean to sanctify this ordinary human life by becoming human himself; the Incarnation of God in Jesus of Nazareth was just some holy smoke-and-mirrors trick.

Furthermore, we've failed to see the glamorization of those apparently successful, have-it-all-together families and churches as something deeply sinister — a temptation to somehow transcend the struggle and pain of being truly human and living on this broken planet. Instead we fantasize about perfect spouses, children, parents, jobs, teachers, pastors, church members. We're quite sure that we must become something other than what we are before we're useful to God, gospel, and Kingdom.

Someone ought to holler, "Fraud!"

The Disciplined Life

Fraud is illegal. It plays footloose and fancy-free with something our lives together can't do without: honesty. The truth is, God accepts and works through real sinners like you and me, *but God never intends us to stay the same.* To say anything less would not only be dishonest, it might breed despair.

One Sunday morning a well-dressed woman in her thirties

approached me after the service. I'll call her Linda. Her daughters fidgeted impatiently beside her as she told me how she'd heard the gospel all over again through the words of the morning hymn:

Just as I am, Thou wilt receive,
Wilt welcome, pardon, cleanse, relieve;
Because Thy promise I believe,
O Lamb of God, I come! I come!

Twenty years earlier, she gave her life to Christ at a Billy Graham crusade. Today, singing "Just As I Am" brought it all back. Over the past two decades her initial enthusiasm had waned. For most of those years she had attended church only on Christmas and Easter. After college she'd started her career, married, then began bearing children. Three kids and two careers left no extra time for something like church. Her husband often traveled, so Sundays were the only real time they had together. Today, he'd taken their son to a Pittsburgh Steelers game.

She said that it was good to be back in church. She liked the message and the hymn; they kindled an awakening. But this awakening would prove different from that twenty years ago. In the words of the hymn she recognized a subtle but very real temptation, a temptation that had damned her for decades to remain among the ranks of busy, self-absorbed, materialistic and often phony upper-middle-class American families with no real time for God or each other. "God accepts me just as I am," she said, "but I'm convinced he doesn't want to leave me there. *I* don't want God to leave me there."

Linda was right. God didn't want to leave her where the gospel found her. She had embraced freedom without obligation, grace without discipline, gospel without law. She came to Christ without a mask or makeup or props . . . "Just As I Am." But there things ended. She never learned to walk. Maybe she was never shown.

At the dawn of a new awakening, what would keep this woman and her family from ordering their lives again around the twin gods of modern America: Me and Money?

From the beginning, Christians learned to balance gospel and law, freedom and obligation, grace and discipline. Immediately following the dramatic response to the gospel communicated by Peter at Pentecost, the church family began to practice their life together: "They devoted themselves to the apostles' teaching and fellowship, to the breaking of bread and the prayers" (Acts 2:42). The early church practiced a disciplined life.

Discipline gives our lives shape, structure, definition, direction. In my family, our evening routine is important for our lives together. It's essentially a discipline. Without such order and discipline, our children would probably become unruly; Julie and I would probably become irresponsible. The church knows this too. From Pentecost onward — at any point in history, in any place on earth — any sustained gathering of Christians has practiced the disciplined life.

Discipline is not legalism. Legalism is a long laundry list of do's and don't's, where our personal security hangs on the successful completion of the list. Legalism worries about right or wrong, good or bad. Discipline, on the other hand, organizes our lives together and trains us for faithfulness. Among legalists, people are either winners or losers. Among disciples, people are only learners. And learning changes lives.

Take the discipline of giving, for example. At an early age, my wife Julie learned that for every dollar she received she was to set aside a dime for God. Today, she leads our family in a regular practice of planned giving to others in the name of Jesus. Sometimes it hurts. Our commitment to giving confronts our desire to own and accumulate. We have to make choices, and sometimes those choices aren't popular. But occasionally they're exhilarating, especially when we see our children learning the joy of giving sacrificially. Disciplined giving liberates us from the materialistic, self-indulgent impulse of American culture and shapes a lifestyle more congruent with the gospel.

Here's a short list of other disciplines to consider:

Prayer — intimate conversation with God, alone and with others.

Common worship — singing songs, dancing, praying, reading Scripture as a family and with the larger church.

Daily work — raking leaves, balancing the checkbook, washing dishes, mowing the lawn, cleaning the house. These ordinary tasks necessary for family life can become acts of devotion if we offer them up to God.

Service — serving others in the name of Jesus: working at a soup kitchen, visiting a nursing home, shoveling snow from a neighbor's driveway.

Solitude — making space to spend time alone and silent before God. Cordless phones, pagers, remote control TVs, VCRs, and stereos make this difficult. Turn them off.

Study — study, meditation, and memorization immerse us in the Bible's message. Don't stop there. Read widely: theology, ethics, history, philosophy, science, poetry, literature, current events.

Celebration — enjoy God, ourselves, each other, and God's creation. It's not hard, for example, to add a festive flair to a dinner or lunch together.

Simplicity — maintain a lifestyle and schedule that promotes faith rather than frenzy. Learn to say "no." Establish a budget and a common calendar. Review it each week . . . *together*.

These are only a handful of spiritual disciplines — those we've found most helpful for our young family. We've found some disciplines either too difficult or too unreasonable to practice at this stage of life. "Fasting," for example, frees us from domination by our appetites. We learn to resist the lure of our consumption-oriented culture. It's an important discipline, but tough to practice when a family has preschoolers who whine and fuss if dinner's running a few minutes late. The practice of the disciplines must be intentional but flexible.

You may want more information about the disciplines. A number of top-notch books are better able to describe them and instruct you in their use. I recommend three: Richard Foster's *The Celebration of Discipline*, Dallas Willard's *The Spirit of the Disciplines*, and, for pastors, Eugene Peterson's *Under the Unpredictable Plant*.

Of Babies, Bunnies, and Missionary Families

Yesterday Kevin and Kim gave birth to their third son. Sean was born in the doctor's office — that doctor's first office delivery in twenty years. Sean's entrance into this world surprised everyone. There was nothing tidy, nothing predictable about it. Later in the day, I visited Kevin and Kim and baby Sean in the hospital. Kevin and Kim were dazed, but elated. Sean slept. Staring incredulously at the child, they recounted the amazing series of events that surrounded his birth. God's gracious care seemed everywhere. Through all the chaos, we glimpsed the hand of God.

I thought back to the birth of each of my two sons. Nothing can compare to the joy I experienced when I cradled them in my arms, and saw them looking up into my eyes, vulnerable, dependent, trusting. But there's nothing on this earth that compares to the way they've radically reshaped our lives together. Their entrance into our lives shattered our well-ordered lifestyles.

During those first few months the boys didn't understand something very important to most of us: nighttime is for sleeping, *day*time is for playing. Initially, they seemed to assume just the opposite. Needless to say, Julie and I spent countless hours rocking them, singing to them, changing diapers, doing everything we possibly could think of to comfort them. Still they cried. Frankly, it frustrated and angered me. Our lives had suffered an invasion of sorts.

Life's that way. A missed meeting, a death in the family, a fight with a loved one, a disgruntled customer, layoffs at work, economic recession, war. Bombarded with the problems of daily living, it's hard to keep ourselves and families from coming unglued.

It's here, in the press of life, that we experience the true test of the disciplined life. Without order our families have no real stability. But without flexibility, the means to bend and adapt, our families will break. Real life is lived somewhere between the rigid and the chaotic.

Oddly enough, God will have it no other way. People and problems invade our lives with annoying frequency. So does God . . . *if we have "ears to hear and eyes to see."*

It's here, in our homes, seven days a week, twenty-four hours a day, that the "communion of saints" is most ruggedly practiced. Here, in our homes, we learn to build families alive to God in our midst; we discipline our ears to hear God speak; we train our eyes to see God act; we teach our hands to reach out, and our lips to speak out in the name of Jesus. While we're at it, we become Real. And yes, it may mean that along the way most of our hair gets rubbed off, our eyes drop out, and we get rather loose in the joints and very shabby. But subtly, often imperceptibly, God moves us from here to there, from selfishness to servanthood, from anger to love, from sinfulness to holiness, from ugliness to beauty.

Once we're Real, we "can't be ugly, except to those who don't understand."

CHAPTER 8

Money Matters:
Toward a Quiet Revolution

THE DRIFTERS came into town not long ago. I confess I didn't know who they were. Born and raised on the high plains of Colorado, I thought a drifter was a cowboy without a home. Julie and I didn't grow up listening to this band from the early 1960s. And by the time we were old enough to enjoy rock and roll, the Drifters had wandered off America's center stage. Decades later in Sharon, Pennsylvania, they walked back on. Hits like *Up on the Roof* and *Under the Boardwalk* helped a crowd of middle-aged Americans remember what it was like to feel the bliss of youthful romance — days before kids and second mortgages and the high demands of vocational responsibility.

The evening began with music by a warm-up band from nearby Pittsburgh. Their job was to break the ice, generate enthusiasm, fuel anticipation. At the high point of their performance, the band belted out the lyrics to the heart-prayer of America's folk religion: "I want money, lots and lots of money," they sang. "I want to be rich, full of love, peace, and happiness!" The crowd sang and clapped and danced in their seats.

But *no one wept*.

The High Cost of Greed

Materialism runs rampant in America. Our culture's values, shaped more by our insatiable consumer appetites than by a biblical vision of creation and redemption, are transforming our churches, our families, and our world. Buying, possessing, and accumulating run roughshod over the virtues of reverence, humility, and simplicity. In our world, economic injustice results in violence, mass starvation, and disease. In America, our foreign policy is often formulated by our international economic interests rather than by a vision of what it means to live together in a global community. The escalating environmental crisis is the product of our blatant exploitation of God's creation, fueled by unchecked economic development.

Yes, money matters. That's merely stating the obvious.

Not long ago, a couple sat in my study, both of them in obvious pain. From their body language, I suspected an affair. They needed help, and didn't know where else to turn. Hank's lips quivered as he told their story. Marilyn fought back tears.

It all started several years ago when Marilyn began working again. Her new job provided a second income, a real boost after years of scrimping and fighting over the smallest purchases. The extra money gave them a new lease on life.

Then came the offers. One credit card after another crammed the mail box. Hank and Marilyn were hooked. For Christmas they treated themselves to a new computer complete with stereo speakers and CD ROM. They added a handful of computer games, and a subscription to America OnLine. Later came a mid-winter trip to Disneyland, a summer vacation in North Carolina, new clothes, appliances. And that was just the beginning: when things got tight, a cash advance from a new credit card helped keep the spending spree alive.

Their passion to enjoy the American Dream couldn't be

satisfied; it refused to be controlled. Within the space of four short years, they tallied up a credit card debt of over $35,000.

I was stunned. I'd prepared myself for the all-too-common confession of marital unfaithfulness — the story of lies and late-night rendezvous and love on the rocks. But this confession blindsided me. Unfortunately, I've grown accustomed to men and women who can't hold sexual desire in check, but I guess I've failed to discern the burgeoning American passion for *things*.

Alarmingly, a growing number of American families find themselves in this kind of debt squeeze. And some of them are us. During the 1980s, consumer debt increased by 140%.[1] By the early 1990s, the typical American household carried $8,570 of non-mortgage personal debt.[2] And in the ten years following 1981, the number of individuals filing for bankruptcy tripled to nearly one million people.[3] The 1980s were a decade of excess. Today, like many American families, Hank and Marilyn and their two children are tasting the sour grapes of an affair with greed.

Most of us don't recognize our greed and deceit until it's too late. In fact, most of us are uncomfortable with those words; we don't like to think of ourselves as greedy and deceitful.

The truth hurts, but the sooner we face the pain, the better.

Where will we find a church that will tell us when we're out of control? Where will we find men, women, and children

---

1. Dana Milbank, "Hooked on Plastic: Middle-Class Family Takes a Harsh Cure for Credit-Card Abuse," *Wall Street Journal* (January 8, 1991), quoted in *All Consuming Passion: Waking Up from the American Dream*, 2nd edn. (Seattle: New Road Map Foundation, 1993), p. 15.

2. Mary Granfield, "Having It All in America Today," *Money* (October 1991), p. 124, quoted in *All Consuming Passion*, p. 15.

3. John H. Cushman, Jr., "Bankruptcy Individuals Are Fewer," *New York Times* (June 28, 1993), quoted in *All Consuming Passion*, p. 15.

honest enough to use words that will wake us from the American Dream? Where are those bold disciples of Jesus Christ, unafraid to say *"Stop!"*?

But that's meddling. And no one wants a church that confronts our foreign policy, criticizes government spending, challenges corporate practices . . . meddles with the family budget. No one wants friends and relatives who poke at our lifestyles. Yet our minds and lifestyles are manipulated, exploited, and shaped by our consumer culture, a culture that often thrives on greed and deceit, a culture whose economic values threaten to destroy us.

We need people to meddle with our lives from time to time. You and I need doctors who are gutsy enough to tell us when we need to change our diets, get more exercise, stop smoking before we kill ourselves. And we need people to tell us when our financial habits lead us recklessly toward danger.

Unfortunately, few American churches and church families honestly wrestle with money matters in light of the new life engendered by the gospel.

God, Mammon, and American Church Families

"When will we stop talking about money?" a church leader asked me during a particularly difficult time with our church budget. "All we talk about is money, giving, and the budget. I'm sick and tired of it. We've got to get on with the real business of the church."

A lot of Christians feel this way when it comes to money. Sometimes I do too. Some of our biggest fights as a church, and as a family, come over money. I'd prefer to avoid them altogether. Sometimes I'd like to get beyond talk about dollars and cents, and move on to the "deeper things" of God and gospel and Kingdom. Though I know that discipleship is intimately related to the way I handle money, I still struggle against the temptation to view money, and all that goes along with it, as a strictly private matter.

Recently, I taught a course on biblical stewardship to our younger adult Sunday School class. Not surprisingly, I learned that only a few of these couples and single parents had written financial plans that they review and revise on a regular basis. Of those that did, still fewer reviewed them with a spouse, and none of them talked about their financial plans with their children. Family financial management is generally a private affair. For the first few weeks, simply talking about money in church made these young adults nervous.

For most American Christians, viewing money, the things money can buy, and our lifestyles as a matter of genuine discipleship is basically uncharted territory. A recent research project brings this dilemma to light. In the early 1990s, Robert Wuthnow, professor of social sciences and director of the Center for the Study of American Religion at Princeton University, amassed data from 175 in-depth interviews and over 2,000 lengthy questionnaires, inquiring into the relationship between religious convictions and economic issues. His primary concern was to study the ways ordinary Americans think about their faith, work, and finances.[4] In 1994, he published his findings in his book *God and Mammon in America*.

This landmark study of American religious values and economic practices suggests that though religious convictions run deep among many Americans, these convictions have little impact on material and economic issues. Stewardship simply isn't part of America's vocabulary.[5] And even among Christians who recognize the term, they define it broadly enough to ef-

4. Robert Wuthnow, *God and Mammon in America* (New York: The Free Press, 1994), p. xiii.
5. Ibid., p. 142.

fectively render the practice of faithful stewardship "so bland that it means very little."[6]

Wuthnow uses one word to describe the relationship between religious faith and economic practice: compartmentalization. For most Americans, religious convictions and money matters belong to two distinct realms that rarely overlap. For example, Wuthnow's study shows that many Americans turn to prayer to help themselves feel better about a new automobile purchase, but few of them stop to consider prayerfully which brand or model they ought to buy.[7]

Prayer, scripture reading, religious values, and convictions belong to the private world of religious devotion. Spirituality functions therapeutically, but has little power to address our daily lives, and our lifestyle choices, prophetically. Says Wuthnow, "we have domesticated [the spiritual realm], stripping the sacred of moral authority and allowing it to break through only occasionally and for good purposes, such as helping us out of a jam or salving our conscience when we succumb to the appeals of Madison Avenue."[8]

Apparently, few Americans feel the need to come to the gospel for financial advice. They feel quite content to divorce matters of money and faith into two separate and distinct worlds. Fewer, still, come to the gospel to have their whole lives rearranged.

This is one thing the God of the Bible won't stand for. An honest reading of the Bible demands that we don't approach the Bible already looking for the message we want to hear, seeking to have our positions, opinions, and lifestyles affirmed. Instead, we come to the Bible to hear the living God speak, to

6. Ibid., p. 145.
7. Ibid., p. 151.
8. Ibid., p. 188.

be addressed, to be *transformed*. Maybe we ought to tremble in the presence of this meddling God.

When we come to Luke's Gospel, for example, there's no skirting the seriousness with which Jesus and the early church handled the whole matter of money. Consider this sampling of Jesus' parables: the Debtors (Luke 7:41-43); the Good Samaritan (10:29-37); the Rich Fool (12:16-21); the Unjust Steward (16:1-8); the Rich Man and Lazarus (16:19-31); the parable of the Talents or Pounds (19:11-27).

Sandwiched between these parables is Jesus' bracing warning: "No slave can serve two masters; for a slave will either hate the one and love the other, or be devoted to one and despise the other. You cannot serve God and [mammon]" (16:13).

Unlike many of the preachers and teachers of his day and ours, Luke views money not necessarily as a sign of God's approval. Money too often poses one of the great dangers to discipleship. The rich young ruler walked away from Jesus because he could not part with his money (18:18-25). Another rich man died a "fool" because he relied too heavily on his ability and his well-stocked barns rather than on the provision and power of God (12:13-21).

Jesus is deadly serious about money and what it can do *for* people and *to* people. That seriousness must be shared by the church — the individuals and families who confess Jesus Christ as Lord, and seek to follow in his steps. And taking God and money seriously means more than attending another Bible study, or hearing another sermon series on stewardship.

Rediscovering the Poor

One hot summer, a handful of adults and a dozen high school kids from our church climbed aboard a rented van and headed south. They went to serve among homeless women and children

115

at the Star of Hope shelter in a rough downtown section of Houston, Texas.

The poverty of the inner city shocked them. For most of them, poverty had long been an idea, a scene from the evening news, a page from a school textbook. But now poverty had a face: poverty became a child who wanted to be held, a mother who needed to talk, a family without a home — sometimes without clothes or food or toys. These middle-class American Christians were overwhelmed. Some of them wanted to go home. Our youth pastor feared he'd made a big mistake.

But by mid-week things began to change. In a private meeting, adults and students began to talk about their fear and frustration, guilt and anger . . . even their trouble understanding God's justice. Talking got things out in the open. They confronted their prejudice, their pride, their ignorance. Over the next few days, these fairly affluent middle-class Presbyterians learned to embrace the poor. They learned to treat the poor and needy as friends, not as objects of charity. On Friday night, as the Star of Hope shelter disappeared in the rearview mirror, kids and adults wept.

A one-week experience among Houston's poor was more effective than any twelve-week course on biblical stewardship, or any autumn stewardship drive. Sorry, pastors. In this matter, poverty may be God's most powerful teacher. This group returned with a new understanding of the economics of discipleship. And the good news is that few of us have to leave our community for this kind of education. The poor are all around us.

Just last week, I arrived at the Prince of Peace Center, a local mission to the poor and disenfranchised in our community, shortly after a young mother had come asking for something for her newborn to sleep in. "A used crib, an old car seat, even a large basket will do," she said. The young woman had delivered the child three weeks earlier, but was unable to bring the baby home from the hospital. The mother's fragile health made the infant's first weeks precarious. Finally strong enough to leave the hospital, the nursing staff had placed the little girl in her mother's arms and wished her well. I wondered if they had whispered a prayer for the child's future.

"I'm glad we had something," says Sister Clare Marie, who helps operate the Prince of Peace Center. "But an old bassinet and a few tattered blankets bring little comfort in the face of such grinding poverty."

Sister Clare Marie and her staff minister courageously here in this western Pennsylvania valley. Once known as an industrial center for the region, our valley is now filled with the tired old relics of our industrial past. Gone are thousands and thousands of jobs. Unemployment soars. So does poverty.

"At times I feel overwhelmed," Sister Clare Marie confesses. "Here, among the poor I learn my own poverty. I am utterly powerless to bring change. God knows we do what we can. We give food, clothing, emergency assistance, counseling . . . anything we have. But most important is the gift of dignity. I've learned that if all I can do is to touch people and speak their names, I've at least granted them a bit of the God-given dignity they deserve." Most of the time, a smile is her only reward.

Poverty surrounds Americans. Urban poverty is a world-wide epidemic. In 1970, 650 million poor people lived in the cities of our world. By 1990, the number of urban poor had soared to 1,650 million, and by the year 2000, analysts expect 2,000 million people in the urban centers of our world to be poor.[9] And these figures do not account for the massive population of poor living outside urban centers.

Most of us are familiar with scenes of emaciated third-world children, bellies swollen from starvation. We may even applaud

9. David B. Barrett, "Annual Statistical Table on Global Mission: 1995," *International Bulletin of Missionary Research* 19.1 (January 1995), p. 25.

the heroic dedication of relief workers. But secretly we wonder if it's worth the effort. If we're honest with ourselves, I think most middle-class Americans don't believe that the poor children in Sudanese refugee camps, or on the streets of Mexico City, are as valuable as their own. Not until we walk among them, touch them, and talk with them, do we realize that these are not just pictures in a magazine. Nor are they merely scenes on the television. No. These are human beings created and loved by God. Their value has nothing to do with their economic or social status, and it has nothing to do with geography.

Like America in general, our congregation lives amid poverty. Week after week, year after year, we meet and worship on the corner of State Street and Sharpsville Avenue — the point of convergence for three county census tracts. The census data provide information we prefer to ignore: 20.9 percent of those living north and east of us live in poverty; 32.3 percent of those south of us are poor; and 47.7 percent of the people just west of us live below the poverty line. That means one out of every three persons I meet in the neighborhoods surrounding our church building is poor. And fifty percent of the children in these neighborhoods belong to single parent families. In one adjacent neighborhood, single-parent households soar to nearly seventy percent.[10]

It wasn't always this way. This downtown corner was once part of a thriving commercial and industrial corridor. State Street was lined with the large Victorian houses of business and civic leaders. The neighborhoods were filled with the homes of fairly contented workers.

Things have changed since then. Obviously, our congrega-

---

10. *Socio-Economic Characteristics: Enterprise Communities Census Tracts for the Cities of Sharon, Hermitage, and Farrell, Pennsylvania,* based upon data from U.S. Census Bureau, 1990 (Sharpsville, PA: Mercer County Planning Commission, 1990).

tion is not blind to the changes. Our Food Pantry ministry helps a handful of those who struggle economically. Our mid-week Youth Club program draws nearly a hundred children from the surrounding neighborhoods. But these ministries serve those who choose to walk through our doors, and they must learn to meet us on *our terms.*

The poor at our doorstep simply are not a priority. The ministry of a large church, which draws most of its members from the more affluent parts of the valley, demands considerable resources. And besides, middle-class Americans have mixed feelings about the poor. When I bring up the subject of the poor, I get strong reactions. Most of us know that handouts to the poor simply keep them dependent on outside help. We resent the welfare approach, but know no other form of ministry to the poor. And though we know the government is not doing a very good job, we prefer to leave the work to Uncle Sam anyway. Others don't want to help the poor. They see the poor not as victims, but as products of their own poor choices. If the poor don't feel the sting of poverty, they won't feel the need to rise above it. Yet another group feels the best way to help the poor is to give them the hope of the gospel. Hope in eternal life may do little to change their present circumstances, but at least eternity looks bright. After all, Jesus told us that the poor would always live among us (Mark 14:7).

Each of these views holds truth. But sadly, we use them to excuse our neglect of the poor. This is nothing short of disobedience, a faithless avoidance of the messianic mission of Jesus, a terribly myopic reading of the Bible.

Those who refuse to close their eyes to the poor around them are learning that the poor are significant to God. They read the Bible and find overwhelming evidence testifying to the immense value God places on the poor. Jim Wallis, for example, a Christian leader who's spent his life bearing witness to the gospel among those on the fringe of human society, observes that the most prominent theme in the Old Testament is idolatry. Second to idolatry is the subject of the poor. It seems that when God gets pushed to the periphery and people worship wrongly, the poor are marginalized, neglected . . . even abused. Says Wallis, "In the New Testament, one out of every sixteen verses is about the poor! In the Gospels, the number is one out of every ten verses; in Luke's Gospel one of every seven, and in the book of James one of every five."[11]

I find it hard to verify his statistics. It's not that I doubt his integrity. Jim Wallis is deeply serious about integrity. He believes that North American Christians have cut the poor out of our Bibles, and by doing so have forfeited the integrity of our witness. Biblical seriousness cannot be left to our statements of faith, but must work its way out in day-by-day obedience. Among affluent Christians, the real test of our fidelity to Scripture is our relationship to the poor.[12] Jesus holds out nothing but judgment for those who fail that test (Matthew 25:45-46).

No, I don't doubt Wallis. I doubt myself. I doubt my ability to see the poor in the Bible because I know my struggle to see the poor around me. But all that's changing. As I build relationships with the poor, the marginalized, and the oppressed in my community and around the world, my eyes are opening . . . not just to the poor, but to the Bible. My Bible is coming together again, and it's exhilarating. No longer can I separate money matters from matters of discipleship. And no longer can I insulate myself from the poor. I'm slowly learning that not only is the Bible filled with references to money, the things money can buy, and the lifestyles we fund with the money we earn, but many of those references have direct bearing on our

11. Jim Wallis, *The Soul of Politics* (New York: The New Press; Orbis Books, 1994), p. 149.
12. Ibid., p. 152.

relationship with the poor of the earth. And I'm not alone. I think the winds of change are beginning to blow.

The Economics of Pentecost

Presbyterians don't talk about Pentecost very much. We're that group of Christians people make jokes about. People call us the "frozen chosen," and make jabs at our penchant for committees and our devotion to *Robert's Rules of Order*. Pentecost is considerably too disorderly for our well-ordered lives. Except for one highly structured Sunday each year, most of us avoid Pentecost entirely. It's messy business. But I wonder if our skillful avoidance of this disruptive invasion by the Holy Spirit is responsible not only for the evangelical apathy, but also for the economic lethargy among our churches and church families.

Pentecost is unavoidable if we're serious about following Jesus. No biblical writer makes this more clear than does Luke. Luke frames the entire mission of Jesus in terms of the poor, neglected, oppressed, and broken. The opening words of Jesus' inaugural address in the synagogue at Nazareth contain Luke's programmatic statement concerning Jesus' mission to reverse the destiny of the poor and outcast.[13] It is a mission inspired and sustained by the Holy Spirit. "The Spirit of the Lord is upon me," proclaimed Jesus, "because he has anointed me to bring good news to the poor. He has sent me to proclaim release to the captives and recovery of sight to the blind, to let the oppressed go free, to proclaim the year of the Lord's favor" (Luke 4:18-19).

Throughout his Gospel, Luke remains intensely preoc-

13. David Bosch, *Transforming Mission: Paradigm Shifts in Theology of Mission* (New York: Orbis Books, 1991), p. 100.

cupied with the person and message of Jesus as the hope of the poor.[14] The poor not only receive Jesus' blessing, but are the chief citizens in God's Kingdom (Luke 6:20); Jesus' evangelistic work among the poor proves that he fulfills Israel's messianic hope (7:22); the poor are among the first seated at Jesus' Great Banquet (14:13, 21); Jesus rewards the poor with salvation and judges the rich (16:19-31); the meager gift of a poor widow far exceeds the ostentatious offerings of the wealthy (21:1-4).

Luke's preoccupation with Jesus and the poor doesn't end with the final pages of his Gospel. Through the post-Pentecost community in the Acts of the Apostles, Luke demonstrates that the same Spirit who anointed Jesus now empowers the church to continue his ministry. Not only is the gospel preached to the poor, the poor experience the gospel in concrete ways . . . so does the whole church. And onlookers are stunned by what they see and hear.

Luke testifies that Pentecost snapped the chains of materialism among the members of God's new family. Buying, accumulating, and possessing no longer held people in bondage. They sold their possessions, gathered the profits, and gave freely to the poor in their midst (Acts 2:44-45). There was not a needy person among them (4:34).

Jewish law called for a land free of poverty (Deuteronomy 15:4-5). In the New Testament church that land now took visible shape among a people whose life together became a visible sign that God was fulfilling his purposes for his people. These individuals and families consecrated everything they had in service to the Kingdom of God, investing themselves and their belongings in God's messianic mission to the world.[15] Their open fellowship with the poor and outcast became the

14. Ibid., p. 98.
15. Jürgen Moltmann, *The Church in the Power of the Spirit* (New York: Harper and Row, 1977), p. 356.

church's protest against the injustice of poverty, a witness to the inbreaking of the Kingdom, and an announcement of God's gracious extension of forgiveness and salvation to all people.

Here is clear and visible evidence: Jesus is still in the world, and the church continues his mission in the power of the Holy Spirit. Is it any wonder that "day by day the Lord added to their number those who were being saved" (Acts 4:47)? Part of the miracle of Pentecost was economic. Evangelism and conversion were a natural consequence.

I'm joining with affluent Christians everywhere, long dissatisfied with the anemic, self-indulgent form of middle-class American discipleship, and praying for a reformation of our biblical integrity, a renewal of our evangelical passion, and a conversion of our economic life together. In short, I'm eager to experience the full blast of the Holy Spirit.

A Quiet Revolution

I fear that some readers will dismiss my words as idealistic and out of touch with reality. My appeal for an economic transformation of family life may sound interesting on paper, but some may say that it ignores the complexities of ordinary, daily life as an American family. This world isn't a utopia, they argue.

I guess I'm not surprised. Through my conversations with people all over the country, I'm learning that most of us assume that the gospel ought to make sense, sound normal, fit into life as we know it. I'm not sure anything could be more misguided. The gospel is the news about Jesus of Nazareth, a Jew executed nearly two millennia ago, getting loose in the world again. As Lesslie Newbigin puts it, "To believe that the crucified Jesus rose from the dead, left an empty tomb, and regrouped his scattered disciples for their world mission can only be the result

123

of a very radical change of mind."[16] The gospel demands not only a radical change in our thinking, but also in our living.

I think that many in the church have stopped believing that ordinary men, women, and children are capable of immensely heroic action. Neither Easter nor Pentecost will allow such faithless dabbling in the rhetoric of what's practical, achievable, or socially acceptable. The new thinking and living engendered by the gospel — the ethics of God's Kingdom — are certainly *not* practical and achievable, at least not apart from a community whose members are in vibrant relationship with both the risen Lord and the poured-out Spirit. And sometimes, such thinking and living will not find acceptance by the larger society. Only the support of genuine community can sustain the heroic actions — the revolutionary ethic — which the gospel inspires. Alone, even our best intentions usually run out of steam.

Various forms of Christian community signal the early signs of this quiet revolution. The grassroot Christian initiatives found among the base Christian communities of Latin America, and the house-church movement current in various hot spots throughout Australia, Great Britain, Korea, and North America, are expressions of this kind of gospel-driven economic change. Many of these communities are based upon a common ethic of accountability that fuels a deeper engagement with God's world than mere charity, or even compassion, can ever provide. They are passionate and persuasive witnesses to the good news of God's salvation revealed in Jesus Christ.

Unfortunately, traditional churches continue to perpetuate the taboo not only against discussing money matters in public, but against allowing the gospel to challenge our financial prac-

16. Lesslie Newbigin, *Truth to Tell: The Gospel as Public Truth* (Grand Rapids: Eerdmans, 1991), pp. 10-11.
17. Wuthnow, *God and Mammon*, p. 150.

tices. Robert Wuthnow says, "Only participation in small, intimate fellowship groups seems to break through this taboo."[17]

Some look to small groups of men, women, and children — related by baptism, not by blood — who gather regularly for fellowship, prayer, worship, study, and mission. I applaud and encourage them. But I can't help thinking that the most basic form of Christian community is found within our nuclear families. Of course, our families are sometimes the last place on earth in which we expect to experience the gospel, but frankly, so is the Christian church . . . or any gathering of Christians, for that matter. A colleague of mine says that he questions the call of those would-be pastors who say that they are entering the pastorate because they enjoy working with people. "I wonder if they've ever really gone to church!" he says. True, Christians are saved, but salvation hasn't necessarily made them easy to get along with.

According to the Apostle Paul, the preaching of the Cross is scandalous to the unconverted mind. Nevertheless, this scandal is God's way of saving the world (1 Corinthians 1:18). I think the same can be said of the church, or any gathering of Christians . . . including the family. It may appear scandalous, but I consider the family God's chief vehicle for inspiring and sustaining this heroic vision of Christian economic revolution.

My heroes are ordinary and not hard to find, if you know where to look. Most of the time, however, they don't think of themselves as heroes. In fact, I often surprise them by suggesting that their lives are extraordinary expressions of the gospel. From their perspective they usually feel closer to failure than to success.

Not long ago, I added another family to my list of heroes.

According to conventional standards, Christmas several years ago was a great success for Dave and Marsha and their three children. Presents littered the floor around the tree; the family was busy with parties and church services; the kids even went caroling at a local nursing home. To top it off, they weren't broke by Christmas Day — thanks to Dave's year-end bonus.

"But Dave and I couldn't ignore a growing discontentment with it all," Marsha told me during an informal discussion around the family's kitchen table. "Each year we've grown to resent what I call the *have-to's* — we *have-to* do this and that, we *have-to* buy this and that, we *have-to* take part in what has become a season of excess."

The following year their family made some changes. They started talking about their budget . . . as a family. Talking about money and how the family spent it wasn't easy at first. Dave was accustomed to handling everything on his own. He wasn't sure he liked answering probing questions from the kids. And Marsha thought the discussions about money might place unnecessary stress on their children. Friends and relatives said that they were playing with fire. But perseverance paid off. Over time it became clear that the children were gaining a healthy respect for money — they no longer behaved as if money grew on trees.

Later they added a brief period of Bible reading and prayer to their weekly "Family Conference." Their reading and praying began to shape these family discussions. Hannah, their youngest, seemed particularly keen at pointing out what the rest of them overlooked. Six-year-olds are still fresh enough to say what's on their minds.

"Daddy, are we rich?" Hannah asked after her father read from Mary's Song in the first chapter of Luke.

"Well, I suppose so," answered Dave, "at least when we compare ourselves with most people around the world. . . ." Dave intended to point out that though their family's resources were rich by some standards, they were rather meager according to others.

"But the Bible says that hungry people get good things,

18. Hannah was referring to Luke 1:53.

but rich people don't get anything from God," Hannah interrupted. "If we're rich, is God mad at us?"[18]

I couldn't help wondering out loud about the way Hannah's parents answered her question. Dave and Marsha said her comment caught them off guard. They'd never seen the passage that way. They'd never really wondered if their lifestyle made God angry. Dave said that Hannah's persistent questions challenged them to do more than merely read the Bible, pray, and talk about the budget. They started setting financial goals consistent with their growing sense of economic discipleship, and they determined to live more simply. One of those goals is worth sharing with a wider audience.

In order to build an awareness of world hunger and to foster the involvement of their children in the worldwide mission of the church, Dave and Marsha and their children prepare a simple meal of rice and beans once a week. After they give thanks for the meal, one member of the family leads the others in prayer for the hungry of a particular country of the world, interceding for the church in that country. Dave uses selections from Patrick Johnstone's *Operation World: The Day-by-Day Guide to Praying for the World.* Dave's abridgment of Johnstone's work gives the family a brief survey of a country's economic, political, and religious life.

Each week, the money they save by eating more simply goes into a section of the family budget labeled "In the Name of Jesus." Then, during the last Family Conference of the month, the whole family identifies a project or agency, either local or international, which will help feed the hungry in the name of Jesus. Dave confessed that the gifts weren't much, but he believes the simple discipline is having a profound impact on the family. "The kids are learning the geographic, political, and religious landscape of the world. They're talking about their faith, and they're putting that faith into action."

I was impressed. But I still wanted to know what kind of

problems they encountered — what kind of issues these changes raised.

"Plenty," said Marsha. "They've caused us some pain and frustration. We've all pouted and whined from time to time. There are things we used to do and buy without question. Now some of those activities and purchases are subject to serious discussion. And those discussions often aren't pleasant."

"I think the changes have been hardest on Brad," Dave mused. "Brad's fourteen, and like any teenager, he faces a lot of pressure from his peers. He needs all the right clothes, expensive shoes, the newest computer games. Marsha says he has a real case of the *have-to's*. I'll be honest, at times we worry that we're alienating him from us, from our Christian convictions . . . even from God.

"About once a week I feel like everything we've worked for will come crashing down around us and we'll slip back into that bland middle-class American lifestyle we hoped to escape.

"But God is faithful. It seems whenever we feel that way, God breaks in and reminds us that we're doing the right thing."

I pressed for details.

"Well," began Dave, "last Thanksgiving we decided it was time to give more than money to the needy in our community, so we went to serve Thanksgiving dinner at a local homeless shelter. Brad wasn't thrilled . . . *at all*. He wanted to eat a big meal and watch football with his buddies. Going to a homeless shelter just wasn't cool. Our Thanksgiving Day started with a great big fight. And I wasn't thrilled. We had to drag Brad along."

I knew the shelter. It's the fruit of a growing missionary partnership between a handful of local churches and an African-American economic development organization. The family was part of a team who offered to serve dinner and spend part of the day with a dozen homeless women and children.

"After dinner," continued Marsha, "Brad flopped down in

front of the television to watch football. He stayed there all afternoon, occasionally chatting about players and teams with a teenage resident named Michael. We didn't talk much at all that day; the morning's fight was a barrier we still hadn't crossed.

"Late that night, Dave and I were getting ready for bed when Bradley knocked on the door of our room.

"'Sorry about this morning. . . . I guess I was kind of a jerk,' he said. We could tell he had more on his mind.

"'Do Michael and his mom really not have a place to live?'

"We told him as much about Michael and his mom as we knew.

"'Maybe we could do something for them . . . I mean, if they don't have anywhere else to go, maybe they could come here for Christmas.'

"As Brad turned and walked down the hallway, Dave and I looked at each other, a little stunned, and *just wept*."

There are signs that Jesus is still loose in the world.

CHAPTER 9

Teaching the Faith:
Disciple-Making Comes Home

I used to want to be a Super Christian.
The reason I stopped pursuing that goal was because
I had no role models.

MelDancer@aol.com[1]

NOT ONE Christian worth imitating. I'm hard pressed to imagine a more stinging indictment against the church in our day than this. I wish it were an isolated case. It's not. "Mel" speaks for an entire generation — a generation more at home talking about God in the electronic chat rooms and message boards on America's information highway than in the Sunday School rooms of traditional churches.

"Mel" is one of roughly 38 million young men and women born between 1963 and 1977, give or take a few years. As a group, we know them as baby busters, twentysomethings, 13th Gen, slackers, whiners, post-boomers, or Generation X. As in-

---

1. Andres Tapia, "Reaching the First Post-Christian Generation," *Christianity Today* (September 12, 1994), p. 23.

dividuals, they're our neighbors, co-workers, children, relatives, and friends. Behind these labels lives a generation shaped by fierce cultural forces that not only strip them of key social mentors, but make them deeply suspicious of anyone in authority.

This generation was raised during one of the most dramatic social transformations in American history. Fifty percent of them experienced the disillusionment of watching their parents divorce. Many of them grew up in homes where both parents worked; some were latchkey kids who came home to an empty house, and learned to fend for themselves. All of them have witnessed the disorienting rise of crime, domestic violence, political and economic instability, moral chaos, the devastation of AIDS, and the scourge of substance abuse. Through it all, parents, teachers, religious leaders, and politicians have all proven less than trustworthy. Moreover, families, schools, churches, and the government have done little to ease their pain, and provide courage and direction for the future.

"Mel" once clung to the hope held out to her in the gospel; she planned to live the heroism inspired by the message she'd heard preached. But unfortunately, she could find no one — *not one, single, ordinary yet heroic Christian* — through whom she could see the gospel *lived*.

Pity. At a time when they most need it, "Mel's" generation is able to identify too few Christians worthy of imitation.

Disciple-Making in Crisis

"Mel's" isn't the first generation to turn its back on Jesus' church. Over the past three decades the membership figures for mainline Christian churches have plummeted. From the mid 1960s into the 1990s, for example, major mainline denominations lost anywhere between nineteen and forty-five percent of their members.[2] Many people wonder why. A recent study goes a long way toward answering that question.

In 1994, a team of sociologists from major American universities produced a landmark study called *Vanishing Boundaries: The Religion of Mainline Protestant Baby Boomers*.[3] Using an extensive telephone survey, the authors gathered data from 500 adults born between 1947 and 1956, and confirmed as members of either the United Presbyterian Church, USA, or the Presbyterian Church, US. They supplemented these surveys with forty in-depth personal interviews.

According to these interviews, few Presbyterians born during these years spent much time as families talking or learning about matters of faith. For most, the Sunday sermon was their only weekly experience with anything pertaining to religion. Few enjoyed family devotions, read the Bible together, or talked about their faith. Some of the respondents remember asking their parents about religion — usually their mothers — but few recall hearing their parents talk together, or initiate any discussion about religion. Their parents talked about the church *as an institution*, but not about God, theology, the Bible, or the Christian life.[4] Time after time, the researchers heard the respondents say something like this: "My father always went to church, but I don't know what he believed because we never talked about religion."[5]

Americans growing up during these years walked away from the church because what was preached and taught there had little effect on the daily lives of those around them, and con-

2. "Sociologists Study Baby Boomers' Apathy about Religion," *The Sharon Herald* [Sharon, PA] (Saturday, September 18, 1993), p. 6.

3. Dean R. Hoge, Benton Johnson, and Donald A. Luidens, *Vanishing Boundaries: The Religion of Mainline Protestant Baby Boomers* (Louisville, KY: Westminster/John Knox Press, 1994).

4. Ibid., p. 115.

5. *The Sharon Herald*, p. 6.

sequently, even less impact on their own day-to-day existence. Key social mentors did little to create an intentional disciple-making environment in order to pass along the faith effectively to yet another generation. They either didn't know they were supposed to, or didn't possess the equipment to make such a transition possible.

Little has changed.

In a land and at a time when Christianity has essentially been the state religion, most of us have simply assumed that one or two hours of exposure to things "Christian" is sufficient to raise good, church-going kids who grow up to participate meaningfully in society. And in a setting like this, too many of us have assumed that America's public school system is adequately reinforcing the values and worldview taught during those few hours each Sunday. Nothing could be further from the truth.

America is not a Christian nation. It's quite possible that it never really was.

The current crisis in disciple-making is perpetuated, in part, because too many American Christians, for too long, have relinquished their responsibility for disciple-making to the formal, institutional setting of the classroom.

But all around me I see glimpses of men, women, and children . . . whole families . . . who are beginning to recognize the sweeping changes in American culture and the new opportunities for evangelical witness. They are not only becoming intentional about disciple-making, they are growing more serious about making disciples *in the home*, as well as at the church. In an increasingly pluralistic culture, which necessitates a new missionary strategy for Christian life and witness in modern America, these families are learning to transform the ordinary aspects of family life into opportunities to teach the faith. And their churches are finding ways to support, equip, and release them to live and witness in the homes, businesses, and schools where these church families live, work, and learn every day.

133

Intentional disciple-making in the home involves at least six areas of family life. Each area contributes in its own way to creating a climate conducive to Christian formation. My list merely suggests ways in which alert families can make teaching the faith a more creative and holistic endeavor.

Marking Time

Amnesia is more than forgetfulness, it's the loss of memory. Those who suffer from amnesia not only forget simple things like phone numbers and street addresses, they can't recall their own names, their parents, spouses, kids, or any of the people, places, and things that provide their sense of identity. Amnesia is not just disorienting, it's debilitating.

I think part of the malady affecting disciple-making in church and family life is just this — a loss of memory. Oh sure, American Christians remember plenty, but I'm not sure what we remember is necessarily shaping ardent, courageous, and faith-filled followers of Jesus Christ.

For example, when it comes to our calendars, New Year's Day, spring break, Memorial Day, summer vacation, Fourth of July, Labor Day, and Halloween stand tall as key days in our lives. But apart from Christmas and Easter, most Christians haven't a clue about other significant Christian seasons like Advent, Epiphany, Lent, and Pentecost. Not only are we unable to locate these seasons on our calendars; we either can't remember what they have to do with the gospel, or never knew in the first place.

"So what?" you say. "Aren't these just formal traditions?"

Yes, they are traditions, but they are traditions for a reason. Throughout the past 2,000 years, the church has found it necessary to fortify the Christian life through rigorous attention to the promise, birth, life, death, and resurrection of Jesus Christ, and the outpouring of the Holy Spirit. It does this not only by immersing itself in the Scriptures, but by making these events part of our lifestyles — a natural rhythm of living and breathing the gospel through each day of every month of the year. Faithful attention to the seasons of the Christian year is a strong remedy to the danger of amnesia, and a strong tonic against the secularism and paganism latent within the church of Jesus Christ.

One retired couple I'm thinking of is no longer forced to knuckle under to the pressure of a commercialized Christmas season. They've chosen to make Christmas a matter of discipleship. While most of the rest of us are frantic with holiday shopping and activities, these two are pondering the wonder of Advent — the promise of Christ's coming into the world, and the certainty of his return. And while most Americans are taking down decorations, returning gifts, wrestling with how to pay for it all, and whooping it up on New Year's Eve, this quiet couple is leisurely soaking in the mystery of the Incarnation. They've learned that when it comes to Christmas, the Christian celebration of the birth of the world's Savior and Lord doesn't end on Christmas Day, it *begins*.

Families serious about the gospel will find that their lives and the integrity of their discipleship are profoundly shaped by the particular calendar they choose to use.

You may want to consult a pastor for more information on ways to begin appropriating the rhythm of the Christian calendar.

Faithful Friendships

Christians do not take friendship lightly. Taking their cue from Jesus, who embraced his followers as his "friends" (John 15:15), the early church identified friendship as a particular characteristic of the fellowship of faith. "The friends send you their

135

greetings," wrote John at the end of his third letter. "Greet the friends there, each by name" (3 John 15).

The type and quality of the friendships that penetrate our homes hold tremendous potential to foster or hinder the development of faith. To most people — especially parents — this is obvious. And it's nothing new: the sages of Israel were careful to instruct the young about the dangers of association with questionable characters (Proverbs 24:1-2), as well as the power of friendship with persons of integrity (Proverbs 18:24).

Most Christians give no thought whatsoever to the purpose and power of our friendships — those relationships we share with believers and non-believers. Too few of us think about their impact on us, and our impact on them.

Dave and Barb are a couple committed to maintaining real friendships with marginally Christian and non-Christian friends. They keep in regular contact with old friends from college. But it's not without some level of anxiety. These friends don't necessarily share the same values. Their interests and lifestyles can be rather rough. Sometimes Barb and Dave worry about the impressions these friends make on their daughter Kaitlyn and their son Christian.

But Dave and Barb also are part of a small group of Christian couples who study Scripture and pray together on a regular basis. And occasionally they pull their growing families together for a day at the lake, an evening barbecue, or a game night. With these "friends" — in the Bible's sense of the word — Dave and Barb can laugh and play, cry and pray.

"Lots of times I find myself concerned about the impact our non-Christian friends are making on our kids," confesses Barb. "But then I remember that they also have a chance to observe the lifestyle and Christian commitment of couples like John and Tracy, and Brian and Kathy. And they get to play with their kids. And I also remember that Jesus was often criticized for being friendly with some pretty questionable people. We can't protect them; nor do we want to. I want them to know what it means to mingle with those Jesus came to save. And I want them to know what it means to enjoy friendships that help them walk with Jesus. I think this is what it means to put our faith into action."

Friendship, for the Christian, is a matter of faithfulness.

Living Liturgically

I set the Bible on his shelf and turned off the light.

"Daddy, let's pray for our day."

Joshua pulled his matching *101 Dalmatians* sheet and comforter closer to his chin, then snuggled his head deeper into the pillow. He's three now, and sure to tell you if you ask him. Jeremy, just over a year and a half, is already sleeping in his crib across the hallway.

"Okay. You dial and I'll hang up," I suggested.

His eyes wide open, staring at the ceiling, he prayed simply. "I love you Jesus. You are my Lord, and I worship you!"

. Direct and genuine, his words caught me off guard. This wasn't his standard, "God, thanks for A.J. Thanks for our Christmas tree. And the lights. And . . ." Stunned, I managed to babble something relatively religious.

Scenes from the evening flashed through my mind. Joshua stood with children of all ages during the children's Christmas pageant. At the close of the service he stood with the others and belted out these words: "Tell the world that Jesus loves you/Tell them you've found a forever friend/You've opened up your heart's door to him/The Love of Jesus has no end."

Well-rehearsed words. The Bible passages were all memorized, as were the songs. They were drilled into young minds by ritual and repetition.

Joshua's performance didn't surprise me. But his prayer

did. These words were utterly unrehearsed, spontaneous. Well-worn, rehearsed words became more than religious babble; they penetrated his heart and gave birth to this expression of heartfelt devotion — this simple confession of faith.

For many contemporary Christians, the words "rite," "ritual," and "liturgy" evoke little more than a yawn. Few Americans recite the Apostles' Creed, for example, with gusto. We denigrate the ceremonial as hopelessly shallow, and dismiss the formal liturgy of traditional Christian worship as the culprit responsible for the anemic discipleship current among most American Christians — the pathetic state of our church's witness.

For many years I, too, hungered for a depth and authenticity beyond the ritual of traditional worship — some release into the Spirit that transcends the rather rigid and dull order of worship that guides us through our Sunday services. Sometimes I've experienced that release — both inside and outside mainline churches. But I've grown to realize that our longing for regular flights into spiritual ecstasy places an unreasonable demand on our intellectual and spiritual equipment. This mistake is what C. S. Lewis identified as "thinking we can do always what we can do sometimes."[6]

Liturgy enables us to do sometimes what we might otherwise not be able to do. Like Joshua's prayer. Ritual and repetition produced a genuine and heartfelt expression of faith. Athletes know this too. Watch any good basketball player approach the free-throw line, a star baseball player step up to the plate, or a champion pole-vaulter stare down the runway. These athletes perform certain rituals that enable them to sink the winning basket, drive home the winning run, or soar to a record height.

Whether we realize it or not, rites, ritual, and liturgy shape

6. C. S. Lewis, *The Joyful Christian* (New York: Macmillan Publishing Co., Inc., 1977), p. 85.

our lives. Christians serious about making disciples of the Lord Jesus ignore them at great peril.

Our boys are older now, and Julie and I fear that we may too easily become more disciplined about the ritual and repetitive carting of our kids to lessons and practices than we are about setting apart time for family worship, prayer, and Scripture memory. But we hope that the church's liturgy, combined with a patient commitment to practicing simple ritual in the home, will give shape to a handful of disciples whose lives express the faith we profess.

Sacred Space

We cannot underestimate the power our environment exerts on the way we make disciples. And we dare not remain ignorant of its influence.

Not long ago I told an older and wiser pastor-friend about the splendor of a new church I'd just visited. I was all excited about what I saw. The building was truly a work of art. My friend, an octogenarian saint-of-sorts, simply replied, "First you shape the building, then the building shapes you." Having led building projects at several of my denomination's largest churches on the West Coast, he knew what he was talking about.

Our environment encourages some behaviors and discourages others, it stimulates some attitudes and stunts others. How we choose to shape the space around us reveals our priorities and values, hopes and dreams. These choices are an expression of our hearts.

Consider our churches for a moment. A sanctuary that boasts a magnificent organ, one that rattles the building, can effectively inspire worshippers to awe and reverence before the living God. But an elevated pulpit and separate choir loft can communicate to a distant congregation, sitting in long, narrow pews, that God is quite removed from the ordinary affairs of their daily lives, and allows for very limited expressions of non-conformity. A worship setting that has many entrances can suggest to seekers that God is easily approached. But if those doors are heavy and closed much of the time, and we prohibit normal activities like eating and drinking, laughing and playing, within that worship space, we perpetuate the sense that the gospel has little influence on who we are outside the building.

Environment is no less influential in our homes. Think about the placement, size, and number of televisions in most American homes. Think, too, about their use. In many homes TVs (*plural!*) drone away all hours of the day and night.

Is there any question about the priorities and values, hopes and dreams that dominate our lives? Is it any wonder that we have trouble making disciples who are shaped more by the priorities and values, hopes and dreams inspired by the Bible and by faithful followers of Jesus Christ throughout the centuries than by Hollywood, Madison Avenue, and Washington, D.C.?

Hear me well. I'm not against television. I'm grateful for the ways I can use TV for entertainment, learning, and teaching, but I'm deeply suspicious of the ways TV wants to *use me*. I'm not suggesting that faithfulness requires families to toss out their televisions (though in some cases that might not be such a bad idea). But I am suggesting that we take a serious look at the effect TV has on the environment we create in our homes.

I think families can think creatively about ways they can foster a sense of the sacred in the space they call home. An attractive world map on a prominent wall can keep us alert to the global mission of the church, and remind us of the needs of men and women and children living in various parts of our world. A garden in the summer, and house plants in the winter can awaken a deeper sense of care and concern for the earth God has commissioned us to keep. Music can encourage prayer and worship, joy and celebration . . . even . . . dare I suggest it? . . . dancing.

Our family room happens to stand adjacent to the kitchen. At one time we wished the builder had put a wall between the two, but he didn't. Gradually, we've come to recognize the blessing of that decision. This one, rather large room is home to most of our activities. Sometimes it's a bit chaotic. In this space children play, parents cook, and our family eats most of our meals. Here we have Bible Time in the morning, and at night, after the boys are in bed, Julie and I talk or pay bills or read. Through it all, something sacred happens in this space. Our environment helps us remember that God is concerned with all the business of life. Discipleship isn't left only for Sundays.

Teachable Moments

Jesus never built a school. And aside from a few trouble-making teaching stints in formal settings, his educational method avoided the classroom. (The academic and religious authorities who controlled both synagogue and Temple weren't much amused by his lectures — they insured he wasn't invited back). Instead, Jesus taught along the road, by the sea, in people's homes, on city streets, standing in a farmer's field.

When it comes to disciple-making, God's school has no walls — in the brick-and-mortar sense, that is. Some of God's most profound lessons come to us *when* we least expect them, *where* we least expect them. That's what Cleopas and another disciple learned as they walked along the dusty road toward Emmaus that first Easter Sunday (Luke 24:13-35). God showed up, opened their minds to understand the Scriptures, and revealed himself to them in the breaking of the bread. And not long after that experience, God showed up among a band of disciples huddled in an upper room, the doors locked against the outside world. In Christ, God walked through the thick walls of their bewildered, frightened, and disillusioned lives and not only taught them, but commissioned them as his witnesses (Luke 24:36-53).

The gospel isn't a collection of nice religious ideas about God, the world, and ourselves that needs the church to keep it alive. The gospel is the news about this odd God who comes and goes as he chooses, breaking into our worlds sometimes subtly, sometimes imperceptibly, and occasionally with earth-shattering power. The gospel means that those of us who have embraced it live in a constant state of expectation. God is on the move. God will meet us anywhere, anytime, anyplace.

Chris Wright is another of my ordinary Christian heroes. He's a husband to Laura, and a father to Micah and Aidan. He's bright, creative, and passionate about Jesus Christ. Chris doesn't like walls. In fact, he probably colored outside the lines when he was a kid. He still does.

Over the past several years he's developed a friendship with a man not all that different from the man the New Testament writers called "the Gerasene Demoniac" (Mark 5:1-20). Bouts of depression and paranoia, fits of confusion, flights into a world of fantasy, and a legion of voices screaming in his brain, isolated Bill from the rest of the world. Though gentle at heart, Bill frightened people.

Chris didn't know whether Bill was demonized or psychotic or some combination of the two. He only knew that somehow, in the person of this troubled man, God was on the move. Chris's obedience not only affected Bill, it affected Chris himself. And it has affected a number of us. But I think I'm struck most by the ways it has affected his five-year-old daughter Micah.

To make a very long story short, Chris not only succeeded in winning Bill's trust; his friendship provided the accountability Bill needed to keep his regular appointments with his psychiatrist. Chris also succeeded in helping Bill move into his own apartment, and establish some sense of responsibility.

Chris and Bill meet on Wednesday afternoons to talk about buying groceries, paying bills, even thinking about what kind of work Bill would like to do. And they talk about God, the Bible, and discipleship.

Because his wife Laura works full-time, Micah often spends her afternoons at the office with Chris. She colors or reads while Chris works. Consequently, over the past year, she's not only watched her daddy work, she's watched him interact with Bill. She's helped Bill move into his apartment. She's listened to the two men talk about budgets and medications, God and groceries. She's learned that nothing and no one is beyond God's reach. And she's seen the power of the gospel loosed in a broken man's life.

The mission of God in this world, and Micah's participation in it, is not something the church hopes she'll learn from a book or a teacher or a course. She's seen it, felt it, breathed it. Odds are . . . she'll live it, too.

At the office and on the street, around the kitchen table and walking in the woods, God's teachable moments break into our lives with amazing frequency and potential. And most of the time, we don't manage them, control them, or orchestrate them. The news that God can reach us and teach us anytime, anywhere, anyway is truly liberating. We need only open our eyes and ears. Teachable moments are more a matter of discernment than discipline.

Imitating Saints

Unlike the disciples of the Jewish rabbis and scribes, or those of the Greek philosophical masters, Jesus' disciples were not called into an intellectual process in which they were to acquire information from Jesus or about Jesus. When Jesus stepped onto the scene of human history, he didn't ask people to master a body of information. He didn't even ask people to agree with his teaching. In fact, he sometimes made it hard to *understand* his teaching, let alone *agree* with it. He still does.

Jesus isn't so interested in information as he is in transformation. And the center for this transformation isn't a place, but a person. Nor is it a curriculum — at the center stands Christ himself. As Will Willimon puts it, discipleship according to Jesus means "learning the moves, walking the walk, following him down the narrow path that he trod. Jesus asked for imitation. He wanted followers, not admirers."[7]

Discipleship is an invitation to imitation.

When Jesus spoke those decisive words, "Follow me!" and wherever and whenever he continues to speak them, he isn't recruiting members for a new Sunday School class. Nor is he winning loyal members to the institutional church. He wants followers — men and women and children willing to redirect their entire lives in radical obedience to Christ's lordship.

Let me say this as gently as possible, but as forcefully as necessary . . . perhaps more forcefully than I am accustomed to speaking or writing. I'm deeply concerned about the evangelical witness of the adult members of much of the American church. Yes, I said witness. Jesus said, "You will be my witnesses" (Acts 1:8). That's a promise. And whether we like it or not, whether we're aware of it or not, we are witnesses. Good or bad. Attractive or unattractive.

I'm not convinced that the witness of today's adult Christians is an entirely positive one. I'm afraid too many young people hear their parents complain about the church, belittle pastors and leaders and teachers, criticize sermons and projects and programs. I think too many of our children see us smile nicely to other church members on Sunday mornings, then snap

---

7. William Willimon, "The Back Page," *Leadership: A Practical Journal for Church Leaders* 14.2 (Spring 1993), p. 146.

at husbands and wives, children and relatives before we've even finished the noon meal. Is it any wonder that our kids, and millions just like them, want nothing to do with us, our values, our Lord and Savior Jesus Christ? Is it any wonder that we have trouble communicating the gospel to the secularists, Hindus, Muslims, Jews, or any of the other religious persons living in our neighborhoods, cities, nation, and world?

Jesus made it quite clear: lives are converted through other lives. There's no escaping the fact that the commitment of future generations to discipleship is contingent upon our ability to point to living examples — practical saints — men and women and children worth imitating. If we can't, I'm afraid we have little to say to this watching world.[8]

I'm praying for more and more American Christians, especially those parents and grandparents whose children and grandchildren watch them with intense interest (believe it or not), to take seriously their responsibility to live lives worthy of imitation. I'm praying for more Christian adults — women and men, single and married, old and young, who worship in our churches, work in our marketplaces, and live in our neighborhoods — who are willing to learn the moves, walk the walk, and follow Jesus down the narrow path he trod. Along this road, participation in worship and Christian education are not added items on an ever-growing "to-do list," things we get around to when we feel sufficiently religious or have the time to act religious. Neither are Bible reading, family devotions, and informal chats about matters of faith.

Maybe what I'm really praying for is simply this: fewer cheap imitations of religious devotion, and more devoted followers of Jesus Christ who are themselves worth imitating. And I'm praying that none of us will think it's too late to start.

8. Ibid., p. 146.

CHAPTER 10

Practicing Forgiveness:
It Runs in the Family

LOVE and forgiveness walk hand in hand. Don't think for a minute that we can enjoy one without the other. Therein lies our trouble: we live in an unforgiving and love-starved world. And our families are no exception. In fact, too many people find love hardest to experience and forgiveness hardest to practice among those we call "family." Not always, of course, but in my part of the world, those families that love freely and forgive regularly are the exception rather than the rule. And what I see and hear about the larger world around me causes me to think that your part of the world is not much different.

Consider Tom. His story is all too common.

One cold November morning I stood in the drizzle beside Tom's wife and boys as he stepped forward and looked one last time into his father's grave. For Tom, his father's death was more than a loss — it was the death of a dream.

As a young man, Tom chose to apply his skill and education in the marketing department of a growing business in Detroit. The job offer came just after graduation from college. He thought it would make his father proud: a big job, in a big city, making big money. But his father didn't see things that way.

146

It was years, long years, before Tom ever learned why.

Shortly after his move to the big city, Tom noticed a change. Dad was colder, more aloof on the phone. Gone were those playful arguments over the Steelers and the Browns. Gone were those long evenings in camp talking about deer and guns and frozen fingers. Gone was Dad's pestering about Tom's grades, his classes, girls. Holiday meals were strained and forced. Dad even seemed angry. He rarely talked, rarely looked at Tom. Tom didn't know why.

"Is Dad having any trouble with the business?" Tom asked his mother one Christmas as they cleaned up the dishes from the dinner table.

"Not that I know of," his mother replied. Even she failed to look Tom in the eye.

"He's so moody. So different. Something's changed. I hardly feel welcome here anymore."

That was the last Christmas Tom spent at home. Several years later, Tom learned the reason for the coldness in the relationship with the man who had once shown him such warmth. Here was a father who had dreamed of working side by side with his son for life; here was a father who had always planned for his son to carry on the family business; here was a father who had sent his son to college with this in mind; here was a father who had lived and worked and saved because of a dream. But Tom had chosen a different path. His dream shattered, this father never forgave his son.

Tom continued to live and work in Detroit. He became quite successful. Tom dreamed too. He dreamed of a day when he and his father and Tom's three sons could argue about the Lions and the Steelers, and could spend long hours in camp together. He dreamed of a day when his father would pester his sons about grades and classes and girls. He dreamed of forgiveness — of a relationship between a father and a son restored.

Now that dream lay dead in the casket with the father who

had loved him once, and who he had hoped could love him again. But this father never forgave his son.

An Unfolding Drama

Among the first stories the Bible tells are stories of alienation. Before the end of the Book's third chapter, sin shatters Eden's harmony, and the first couple hides from God. By the end of the fourth, sin leads to violence, leaving Abel dead and Cain a fugitive. Lest those who read the first few chapters of the Bible become too enamored with the marvel of the cosmos, the beauty of the earth, and the goodness of humankind, these two stories quickly lower a dark and sinister backdrop against which the bright and hope-filled drama of reconciliation will soon dance.

Consider the story of Cain and Abel (Genesis 4:1-16). Within the span of sixteen terse verses, this story moves from a situation of stable family life to an experience of unresolved alienation.[1] This part of the Bible reads like any of number of modern newspapers: "Mother Drowns Children," "Wife Dismembers Husband," "Brothers Murder Parents," "Husband Accused of Double Slaying." All these stories are tragic, but according to the Bible they're nothing new. In the beginning, Cain murdered his brother — not a member of another tribe or race or nation. The victim was his own flesh and blood . . . *family*.

Here in the Bible's first story of violence — *domestic violence* — the storyteller is not so much interested in telling us that murder is a bad thing.[2] The world knows that much. This

1. Walter Brueggemann, *Genesis*, Interpretation Series (Atlanta: John Knox Press, 1982), p. 54.
2. Ibid., p. 55.

narrator tells about about Cain and Abel in order to describe the force that ravages the world, clawing and maiming its victims. Sin lies in ambush at the heart's door, waiting to leap upon its victim. It's violent. Furthermore, it's fatal. Once conquered, a person's destiny is haunted by sin; not only are relationships with others twisted, so is the relationship with the Maker.

This story of treachery within the first family begins the Bible's extended struggle with the problems of life lived in relationship with others, particularly family. It's a commentary on an ancient and perennial human dilemma: life alone is hard enough, but life lived together with others can be downright impossible . . . even dangerous.

From the beginning, the Bible is clear: sin is terrible. Human beings — even members of the same family — will violate one another, and reconciliation will appear impossible. But that's not the end of the story.

Halfway through this short episode, Cain himself is as good as dead: "My punishment is greater than I can bear!" (Genesis 4:13). Alienation does that. Anyone whose actions have deeply hurt a parent, child, spouse, or friend knows the pain. And few of us need God to punish us; we're plenty good at punishing ourselves. Instead, God promises to guard Cain's life. The promise is a whisper of hope. God hasn't give up on sinners — even those who murder their brothers. We hope that sin and death and evil may not have the last word after all.

Within the book of Genesis, the story of Abel's murder by his brother Cain foreshadows the stories of Jacob and Esau, and Joseph and his brothers. More broadly, it sets up the message of the Bible.

As the larger Story unfolds, we watch Jacob and Esau marching toward one another. We know this story of treachery and deceit, and we fear a blood bath. But the story turns. The unexpected happens. Esau forgives his brother. They embrace.

149

Here's an unmistakable sign: sin isn't the only force loose in the world.

A few pages more, and we watch Joseph the bureaucrat toy with his brothers as they grovel for grain. Again, we know the story of envy and hatred, treachery and deceit. And we know that Joseph has reason to judge them; we know that he has ample authority to punish them. They deserve his wrath. And if we had read this story in isolation, we would expect retribution. But our reading of Genesis has altered our expectations, tempered our understanding of justice. The story of Jacob and Esau proved that sin isn't the only force loose in the world — *so is grace*. And we've begun to wonder which is the more powerful of the two. Joseph's act is decisive: he opens wide his heart and extends his arms to the brothers who hated and hurt him: "Even though you intended to do harm to me, God intended it for good. . . . So have no fear; I myself will provide for you and your little ones" (Genesis 50:20-21).

There's no question now. Though sin is loose in this world, it doesn't need to lead to violence and bloodshed. Differences are not irreconcilable. Grace, expressed through forgiveness and directed toward reconciliation, is also at work in the world.

The Bible's early stories of alienation and reconciliation provide a motif that weaves its way throughout the Scriptures. Into the dark and sinister silence of primal estrangement, God whispers the bright promise of reconciliation — with each other, and with God.

Later, much later in the Story, we stand among the crowds on a dark afternoon and watch Jesus die on a cross. Human cruelty has taken on a devilish twist, and this is the Bible's darkest day. Tried unjustly, condemned mercilessly, beaten, ridiculed, and crucified, the man who promised so much has become the victim of that violence which first entered this world long ago through Cain's hatred — hatred that now appears to run unchecked. If ever we are ready to abandon all

150

hope and curse this cruel world, it's now. But into this dark and sinister silence, we hear another whisper: "Father, forgive them," Jesus prays. "For they do not know what they are doing" (Luke 23:34).

No, they didn't know what they were doing. But we know. We know that the life, death, resurrection, and mission of Jesus Christ complete that promise whispered long ago. God hasn't given up on this world, a world that so often seems to be hurtling recklessly toward disaster. We know the end of the Story. Sin and death and evil won't have the last word. God will. Judged and banished forever, sin and death and evil will no longer haunt our lives. God will straighten twisted relationships; God will restore the bliss of that friendship once enjoyed between his creatures and himself; God will transform the discord of the entire broken creation into a marvelous symphonic harmony (Revelation 22:1-5).

In this, the Bible's final vision, we see paradise restored. But it's not exactly what it was at the Beginning. Things have changed . . . for the better. Adam and Eve produced a vast mosaic of families; the Garden has become a city.

A *city*. Imagine that! New York, São Paulo, London, Rome, Moscow, Cairo, Jerusalem, Calcutta, Bangkok, Hong Kong, Seoul, Mexico City . . . the great urban jungles of our world, and their vast array of peoples and problems, transformed into one massive human community of praise . . . men, women, and children of all nations and races, tribes and languages gathered together in common worship before the living God — Father, Son, and Holy Spirit!

With eyes fixed on this vision, Jesus endured the cross and prayed, "Father, forgive them." This same hope inspired the Apostle Paul, who endured intense suffering, and spread the message of God's reconciling love throughout the ancient Roman world: "In Christ God was reconciling the world to himself, not counting their trespasses against them, and entrusting the message of reconciliation to us" (2 Corinthians 5:19).

Yes, we know what happened that dark afternoon when Jesus, in obedience to the Father, lay down his life to reconcile this broken world.

We know that this Father forgives. So do his children. It seems to run in the family.

Hope for a Broken World

Jim was uncomfortable with his wife's growing friendship with Lou. Lou was friendly, interesting, and self-employed — a regular customer at the coffee shop where Carol worked part-time. Lou usually sat at the counter while Carol bustled to serve a steady stream of customers. It wasn't a terribly busy place, so Carol could usually carry on some form of conversation with Lou. He was never in a hurry. She liked that. And he could talk about anything — travel, religion, politics. She liked that too. His talk lifted her out of the humdrum of her everyday life.

In the months that followed, she spent more time with Lou. They talked on the phone. She went to his home for coffee. Carol enjoyed the friendship. But because she knew her husband's discomfort, she stopped telling him about her chats with Lou.

Most often, Lou talked about his wife. He'd lost her to cancer several years earlier, and the wounds were still fresh. Her listening ear was therapeutic. Carol talked too. She told Lou about her children, her husband, her hopes and fears.

And so, time passed.

Late one evening Jim's uneasiness turned into panic. Jim had stayed home one Friday night with the children so that Carol could go to a women's gathering at church. Partway through the evening Jim realized that he needed to ask Carol about the dosage for their youngest daughter's medication. He phoned the church. Carol wasn't there. In fact, she'd never been there.

Jim was worried. He called several of her friends. No one had seen Carol. When Carol walked through the door around ten o'clock, the youngest children were asleep, the oldest downstairs watching TV. She was met by Jim, his face white as a sheet.

"Carol, I tried to reach you at the church. I forgot your instructions about Marie's medication . . . *where have you been?*"

Long pause. They searched one another's eyes.

"Would you be upset if I told you I was at Lou's for dinner?"

"Carol . . ."

Her words hit him like a ton of bricks. She'd lied to him. She'd intentionally set up the whole evening behind his back. Jim was crushed. Carol fled to the bedroom in tears. Jim wondered how much time she'd spent with Lou over the past months — how often she'd deceived him. Carol wondered how Jim would react if he knew the truth.

The next few days were difficult. But they talked, and talking helped them dismantle large sections of the wall that stood between them. Carol was sorry for lying. She was sorry for introducing distrust into her relationship with the one person who had trusted her completely. She worried that she might never rebuild the trust their marriage once enjoyed — especially if she told Jim the whole truth. She toyed with leaving parts of the wall intact. She nearly convinced herself that it was wiser to keep the truth from Jim, and bear the pain alone rather than hurt her husband further. Besides, she didn't know how he'd react. She could bear her secret pain, but she couldn't bear to live without her husband's love.

But the secret tore her apart inside. After a few torturous weeks, Carol decided she could keep it from Jim no longer. So, late one evening, after the kids were in bed, Carol mustered up enough courage to tell Jim there was still something he didn't know.

"Jim . . . there's more . . ."

"You slept with him." He spoke the words haltingly in disbelief.

"Yes."

Jim buried his head in his hands.

"Once?"

"No . . . Jim, I'm so sorry . . ."

Jim turned and walked out the door.

A week later Carol came to see me. Through tears she retold the story. She told me that Jim liked and respected me, and asked if I'd talk to him — she'd heard he was staying at a local motel.

I met with Jim and found him not so much angry as hurt. He felt violated, used, betrayed. Sure he was mad — he was mad at Lou, he was mad at Carol, he was mad at himself. But it was his pain that isolated, even paralyzed him.

"Pastor, the pain just runs so damn deep," Jim told me. "I can't shake it. Do you think I like living here away from Carol? I hate it. I want to be with her. I want to hold her again. But I don't know what to do with the pain."

Out loud, I wondered if he would be willing for the three of us to meet. We could talk, pray, chart a course for rebuilding their shattered lives. He agreed.

The months that followed were anything but easy. Carol was haunted by guilt. Jim experienced fits of rage. Both moved in and out of depression.

There are some things in life that are easier to overcome than others. But as Lewis Smedes says, "The deep pain of broken trust has one cure, only one. It is the remedy called forgiveness."[3]

3. Lewis Smedes, *Caring and Commitment: Learning to Live the Love We Promise* (New York: Harper and Row, 1988), p. 121.

And I suspect that there may be no other experience in which trust is more violated than in the painful case of marital infidelity. "Adultery slices so fiercely into the tender tissues of trust," continues Smedes, "that we can go on with our commitment only after our injured spirit agrees to the soul surgery we call forgiveness."[4]

Jim and Carol not only agreed to such "soul surgery," they learned to practice it.

Some of Jim's coworkers thought he was foolish. They told him that he was too easy on her, and they predicted she'd hurt him again. One Christian even suggested that Jim had justification for divorce; after all, Jesus allowed for divorce in the case of adultery.

This was a genuine test of faith. In an age and culture fractured by irreconcilable differences, was the ethic inspired by the gospel anything more than wishful thinking? Can forgiveness lead to reconciliation?

Eight months after my first meeting with them, we gathered with a small group of family and friends for a renewal of their marriage covenant. On their fifteenth wedding anniversary they spoke their old vows with a far more profound sense of commitment and meaning than that day long ago when they spoke them with misty-eyed innocence.

In the case of Jim and Carol, forgiveness not only cleansed, it healed a deep and potentially fatal wound.

But you need to know this, Jim and Carol didn't walk this path alone. They were surrounded by a small band of believers who helped them remember the gospel even when they had difficulty remembering it themselves. The support of this genuine Christian community helped birth and sustain this heroic act of forgiveness and reconciliation that continues to bear witness to the gospel.

4. Ibid.

Left to themselves, isolated by their guilt and pain, Jim and Carol may well have become more of sin's victims. Instead, they have become a living testimony to the gospel — a sign that Jesus is still loose in the world, forgiving and reconciling, and using ordinary people to announce the news to the world.

There's hope for this broken world.

Practicing What We Preach

Jim and Carol aren't the only ones through whom we see signs of Jesus' work among us. There are plenty of others. Some of them overcome tremendous obstacles, others minor ones. And for every person who practices forgiveness, I see several others who fall flat on their faces.

Forgiveness needs practice, and there are certain lessons we can glean from those who have learned to practice forgiveness well. I've watched plenty walk through the pain of relational brokenness, and I've learned to bear my own share of such pain. Here's some of the wisdom I've gleaned . . .

Lesson One: Cultivate Humility

Humility is a conscious awareness of my own shortcomings. For the Christian, it's the fruit of an honest appraisal of the betrayer within, a recognition of my brokenness — my propensity toward sinfulness. Sin is not another person's problem; it's mine. Standing before the Cross, I embrace my constant need of forgiveness . . . from God, and from others. Wesley's great hymn "And Can It Be?" is a powerful tonic for that insidious pride still living within my bones. I'm learning that as I deepen my sense of humility, I forgive others naturally.

156

Lesson Two: Live Reverently

Reverence is more than showing respect; I can show people respect, yet curse them under my breath. I'm talking about stopping long enough before a flower or a child, a sunset or a convenience store clerk in order to recognize the wonder and dignity of God's creation. I'm talking about those tragically rare experiences of worship that make me tremble, when I find myself awestruck and dumbfounded, bewildered . . . but strangely warmed.

Too many of us live in this small, cramped world of the self. Reverence breaks us free and ushers us into the largeness of God. Here we surrender . . . no, abandon ourselves to the grandeur of God. I'm learning that as I heighten my sense of reverence, I forgive others consistently.

Lesson Three: Pursue Vulnerability

Ah, now this is a trick for most Americans. We are people intoxicated with power, success, and speed. Is it any wonder that forgiveness is rare? Forgiveness demands vulnerability. When I ask for forgiveness, I must drop my guard, expose myself, admit my failure. And when I grant forgiveness, I must hold another's heart in trust — tenderly, mercifully, lovingly. These deep transactions of the heart never happen in a hurry. They demand trust, and trust takes time to build. When I pursue vulnerability, I will surrender power, embrace failure . . . *slow down.*

Lesson Four: Practice Honesty

The kind of trust I'm talking about is fragile. When someone breaks my trust, or when I drag others through the mud of my

deceit, the only remedy is the truth. Secrets are flimsy founda-
tions for rebuilding broken relationships. I can't forgive what I
don't know. And asking another person to forgive my half-truth
is a sham. Secrets, even ones kept for the good of others, are
dangerous.

I've learned that when you forgive,

> You hold out your hand
> to someone who did you wrong,
> and you say: "Come on back,
> I want to be your friend again."
> But when they take your hand
> and cross over the invisible wall
> that their wrong and your pain
> built between you,
> they need to carry something with them
> as the price of their ticket
> to your second journey together. . . .
> What must they bring?
> They must bring truthfulness.
> Without truthfulness, your reunion is humbug,
> your coming together is false.[5]

Truthfulness is the pledge that proves our willingness to
walk the difficult and often painful road through forgiveness,
toward reconciliation.

Lesson Five: Exercise Discipline

The grace released through forgiveness is a gift, but it's not
without cost — this grace will cost me my life *as I know it*. I'm
not forgiven so that I can go on doing the same old things that

5. Ibid., p. 125.

got me into trouble in the first place. And I don't forgive others in order to grant them license to screw things up again. I'm forgiven in order to start over. I forgive in order to release others to rebuild their broken lives. We hope for conversion, reformation . . . *transformation*. Anything less makes forgiveness cheap.

Dietrich Bonhoeffer loathed what he called cheap grace. "Cheap grace," wrote Bonhoeffer, "is the preaching of forgiveness without requiring repentance, baptism without church discipline, Communion without confession, absolution without personal confession."[6] If forgiveness is going to direct us toward the reconciliation we crave, we will exercise a dogged discipline that puts structures in place that will eventually stabilize the lessons learned through failure.

Lesson Six: Stay Connected

Sin and brokenness isolate. Rare is the person who wants to come to church when she's hurting. And rare is the person who faithfully keeps in contact with his friend who's struggling just to see the light of day. Maybe I'm having trouble, real trouble, believing I'm forgiven. During a time like this, I need others to look me in the eye, and speak those words again . . . and again . . . and again: "In Christ, you are forgiven." Maybe I'm having the same kind of trouble forgiving one who's hurt me deeply. At a time like this, I need someone who's going to listen to my rage, pray over me, and walk beside me.

We cannot walk this path alone. Jesus gave us the church. And it's in the church — among the individuals and families *connected* by faith — that we learn to practice that particular gospel-heroism which we call forgiveness.

6. Dietrich Bonhoeffer, *The Cost of Discipleship*, rev. and unabridged edn. (New York: Macmillan, 1963), p. 47.

Ethics, Mission, and Evangelism

I'm closing this book with a chapter on forgiveness not as an afterthought, but as the goal toward which my thinking and praying and writing presses. There's nothing novel in my approach. I think the Gospel writer John did the same thing. Toward the end of his book, John shows Jesus breathing out the Holy Spirit on the church, and sending them in his name to practice forgiveness (John 20:21-23).

Practicing forgiveness isn't just some handy strategy for building happy and healthy families, which are the envy of the neighborhood. No, practicing forgiveness transforms families into transforming witnesses to the good news of God's justice and salvation revealed in Jesus Christ through the power of the Holy Spirit. Whenever we practice what we preach, mission is inevitable, and evangelism spontaneous.

As things now stand, I find most Americans more apathetic to the Christian message than hostile to it. Throughout the book, I've repeatedly argued that the doors are wide open for the church to live and proclaim the gospel with passion and integrity. Passion is important enough, but integrity is essential . . . especially in our day. People are wary of promises without substance. In a society of skeptics, the gospel is made credible in the face of unbelief by men, women, and children who not only believe the message, but live it. And since the gospel message centers on the One who laid down his life to reconcile this war-torn world, I'm convinced that there's no better way to make the gospel credible than by practicing forgiveness and working for reconciliation.

The gospel is communicated, ultimately, in its practice.